Time for HOMEWORK

Paul
Nightingale

2

Book 2

HUNTER
EDUCATION
NIGHTINGALE

HUNTER EDUCATION NIGHTINGALE

Time for Homework - Book 2

Published by:
Hunter Education Nightingale
ABN: 69 055 798 626
PO Box 547
Warners Bay NSW 2282
Ph: 0417 658 777
email: sales@huntereducationnightingale.com.au
paul@huntereducationnightingale.com.au
www.huntereducationnightingale.com.au

Cover Design: Doriana Berkovic

National Library of Australia Card No.
and ISBN 978 - 1 - 922242 - 26 - 6

Time for Homework
Book 2

Time for Homework Book 2 is the third in a series of seven books written to help reinforce many of the concepts, skills and understanding needed with today's school curriculum. The series is designed as a user friendly resource that treats reading, handwriting, spelling, grammar, writing and mathematics.

The book contains 30 units of work. Each unit can be attempted over the period of one week. Each unit addresses the subjects outlined above along with topics addressed in today's environment and those in the new Australian Curriculum for Mathematics and English.

As the child's skills develop with sounds, words and reading the book introduces stories. They help in the development of word families, spelling and understanding of written texts. In addition the child is introduced to comprehension, punctuation and some grammar. At all times there is an emphasis on spelling, word association and reading.

While *Time for Homework* treats many of the topics presented in the school curriculum, it is a summary of those subjects. This book is fun to use at home for the child in the first year of school. *Time for Homework* is a resource that will help develop learning.

Message to Parents

With *Time for Homework Book 2* you may need to help with explanation of instructions. As a parent you are asked to help with this skill, but please resist the temptation to actually provide answers. Help with explanation, where necessary and assist when needed. As your child works through the book your help will be required less. Reading, maths, handwriting spelling skills, grammar and knowledge of English will develop allowing the child to become a more independent learner with an understanding of the topics treated.

Regular homework helps develop skills in the subject areas treated and confidence in your child with learning which is essential for a good education.

Praise your child at all times, because you are the ideal support person in your child's life. Working together will help with the use of this book. It will help make the learning process more meaningful for you both. *Time for Homework Book 2* is designed as a fun book to use at home. Enjoy the journey!

Reading

At the Zoo

Most big cities have a zoo. A zoo is home to lots of different animals. Each animal has its own special place to live that is like it's real home in the jungle, desert or plain.

In most big city zoos you can see huge elephants, tiny mice, wild lions and tigers as well as gentle lambs and cute monkeys.

You might see seals swimming, or zebras trotting and the family of apes playing.

My favourite zoo animal is the giraffe. They are so tall.

Understanding

Colour the bubble that best fits each sentence ending.

a. Zoos are the home
- ◯ where animals want to live.
- ◯ of different animals.

b. At the zoo you might see
- ◯ gentle lambs and cute monkeys.
- ◯ people swimming with the animals.

c. The animal homes at the zoo
- ◯ are like the real homes in the jungle or plain.
- ◯ for the sick animals.

Interpreting

Answer yes or no to these questions.

a. Do big cities have zoos? ______

b. Do all zoos have special places for animals to live? ______

c. Are all zoo animals cute? ______

d. Do zebras swim? ______

Grammar

Nouns are words that name things. Discuss these nouns, then label each picture. Word bank will help you.

a.

______

b.

______

c.

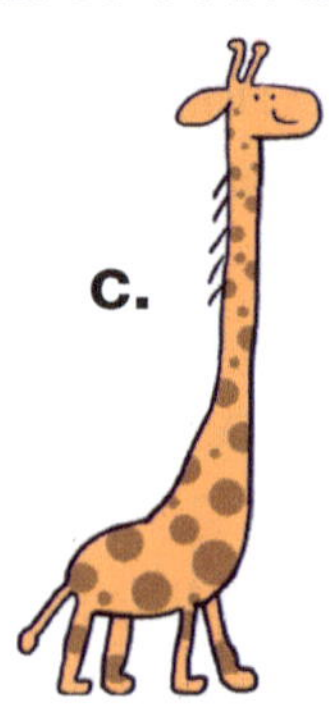

d.

______

e.

______

f.

______ ______

g.

______

Word Bank
- zoo
- elephant
- lamb
- monkey
- zebra
- giraffe
- telephone
- lion
- kangaroo

Unit 1

Spelling

Look, cover, write, check each word.

word	write	check
animal	______	☐
special	______	☐
kangaroo	______	☐
monkey	______	☐
tiger	______	☐
entry	______	☐
fence	______	☐
gentle	______	☐

Word Building

Add the missing sound to build words.

oo

t __ __ k

b __ __ k

h __ __ k

c __ __ k

l __ __ k

r __ __ k

w __ __ l

sh __ __ k

st __ __ d

w __ __ d

f __ __ t

Sentences

Unjumble these words to write sentences.

a. sat back. Amy elephant's the on ______

b. nursed lamb. Paris a baby ______

c. with We animals. lunch had the ______

d. visit zoo class Our the might ______

Counting On

Use each number line to 'count on' for addition.

a.

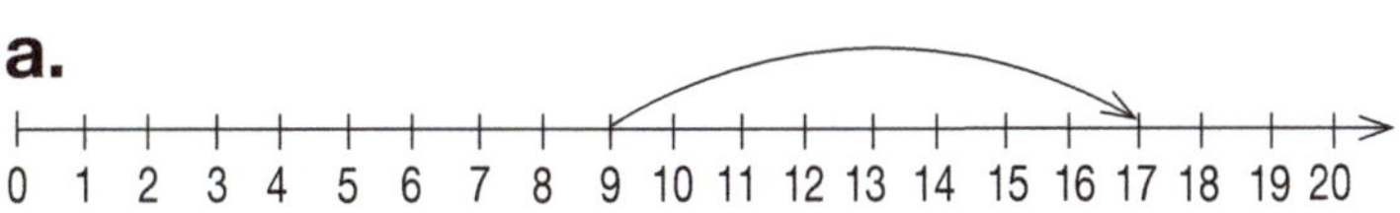

☐ + ☐ = ☐

b.

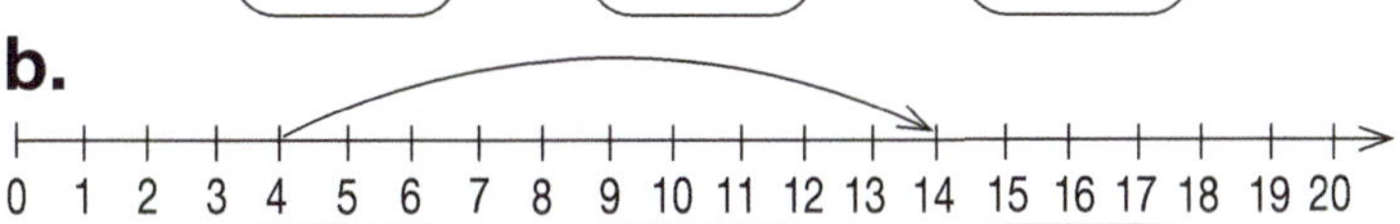

☐ + ☐ = ☐

c.

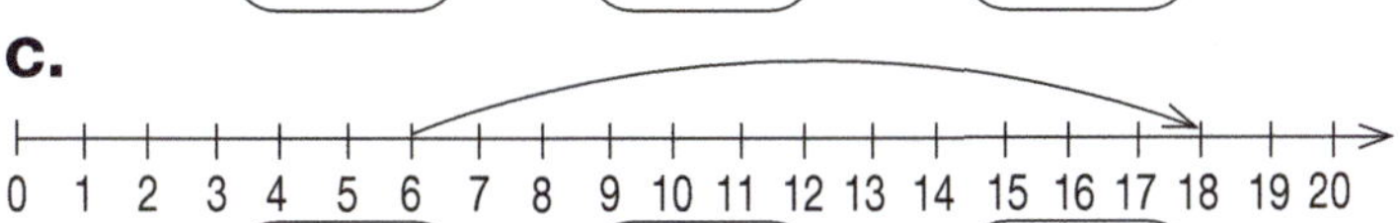

☐ + ☐ = ☐

Numbers 1-100

1. Add the missing numbers.

a. 2, 4, ☐, 8, 10, ☐, 14

b. 3, 6, 9, ☐, 15, ☐, 21

2. Write the number shown on each abacus.

a.

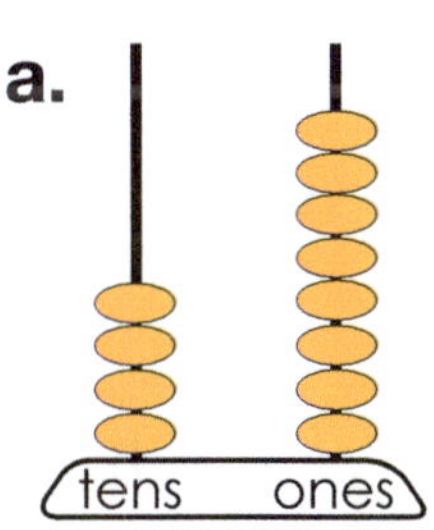

☐

b.

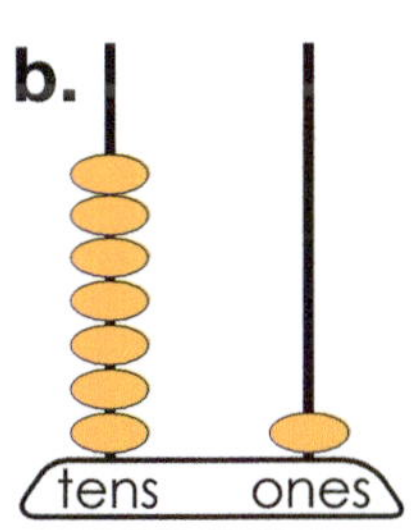

☐

c.

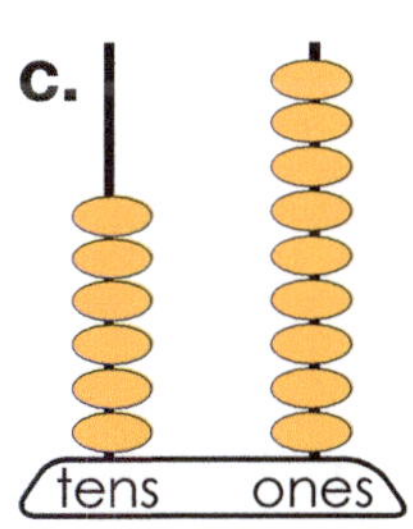

☐

My Home

My family and I live in a caravan. It has a kitchen, shower, toilet and a big annex where my brother and I sleep. Mum cooks all our food on the gas stove or on the BBQ outside. She lets Will and I put our nachos in the microwave to melt the cheese.

There are lots of other children living in the caravan park. Most of them go to my school. We catch the bus near the office every day. The bus brings us home about four o'clock. The bus is always noisy until we get near our stop. Everyone is quiet then because the park manager gets upset if we make too much noise.

Understanding Colour the bubble that best fits each sentence ending.

a. My family live in
- ◯ a caravan.
- ◯ a house.

b. Mum cooks our meals
- ◯ in a microwave.
- ◯ on a gas stove.

c. There are lots of other kids
- ◯ who catch the bus.
- ◯ are noisy around the park.

d. We arrive home
- ◯ on the bus about 4pm.
- ◯ to make nachos.

Interpreting Complete these sentences about My Home.

a. My brother and I sleep ______________________________

b. Everyone on the bus is quiet because ______________________________

c. The bus picks us up for school ______________________________

Grammar Verbs can be "doing" or "action" words. Use these verbs for action.

spread   close   cut   open

a. ___ ___ ___ ___ ___ the fridge door, please.

b. ___ ___ ___ ___ the window.

c. ___ ___ ___ ___ ___ ___ the butter on your sandwich.

d. ___ ___ ___ the sandwich into quarters.

Unit 2 Spelling

Look, cover, write, check each word.

word	write	check
kitchen	______________	☐
outside	______________	☐
where	______________	☐
catch	______________	☐
quiet	______________	☐
much	______________	☐
because	______________	☐
office	______________	☐

Word Building

Add the missing **oo** sound. This **oo** makes a different sound to Unit 1 **oo**.

oo

f __ __ l

t __ __ l

p __ __ l

s __ __ n

m __ __ n

r __ __ m

sp __ __ n

br __ __ m

sch __ __ l

Punctuation

Rewrite the days of the week. Each day begins with a capital letter.

sunday ______________ monday ______________ tuesday ______________

wednesday ______________ thursday ______________

friday ______________ saturday ______________

3D Objects

Match the everyday objects to its 3D name.

a. 

b. 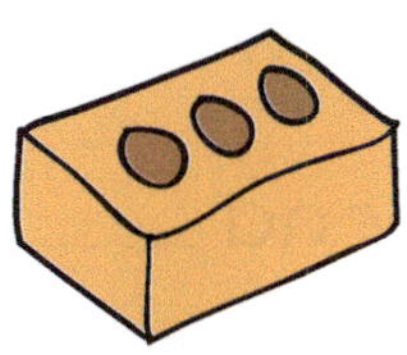

c. 

d. 

e. 

f. 

g. 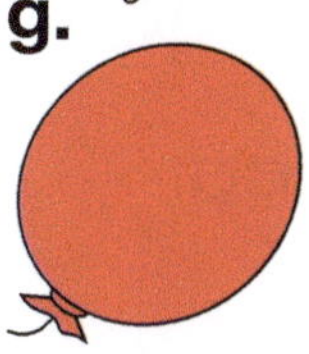

h. 

cylinder

cone

cube

sphere

rectangular prism

Location

Draw these shapes in the correct box in the puzzle.

start here

○ Forward 4, up 3.

□ Forward 2, up 4, left 1.

△ up 3, 3 right.

⬡ up 4, right 2, down 2.

Bike Safety

Most children own a bicycle, and those who don't, usually borrow someone else's to go for a ride.

When you ride a bike, don't be silly and not wear a helmet. If you have an accident or fall off the bike and hit your head, a major injury could result.

It is now law that everyone who rides a bicycle must wear a helmet, so always make sure your helmet fits tightly before you start to ride.

Safety rules are also important for bike riders. Common sense and care at all times will help keep you safe.

Understanding Colour the bubble that best fits each sentence ending.

a. You should wear a helmet
- ◯ because it looks good.
- ◯ to protect your head.

b. If you don't have a bike
- ◯ buy one.
- ◯ borrow someone else's.

c. Helmets must be worn
- ◯ because it is the law.
- ◯ to stop accidents.

d. Bike riders should always use
- ◯ common sense.
- ◯ ride on the footpath.

Interpreting Complete these sentences about bike safety.

a. Make sure your helmet ____________________

b. It is important for bike riders to follow ____________________

c. To keep safe and protect your head ____________________

Grammar Adjectives tell us more about or describe nouns. Colour the path that best describe each noun.

a. green / blue → sky

b. green / pink → grass

c. fluffy / old → clouds

d. big / orange → dog

e. tall / fat → building

f. flat / fast → car

Unit 3

Spelling

Look, cover, write, check each word.

word	write	check
children		
ride		
have		
before		
bicycle		
start		
time		
could		

Word Building

Add the missing **aw** sound to build the words.

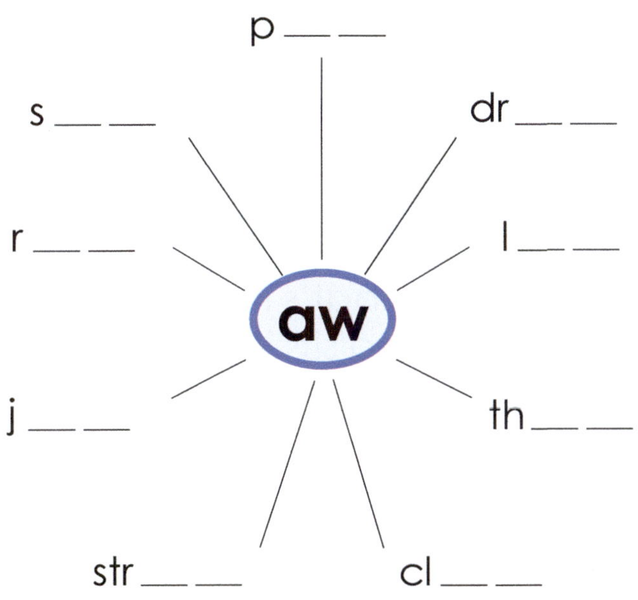

Road Safety

Write what you do at each sign when riding a bike.

a. 

b. 

c. 

d. 

Time

1. What time is it?

a. 

b. 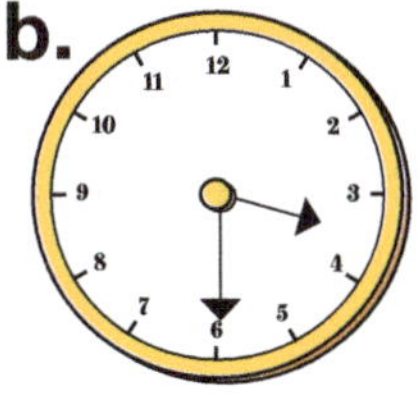

c. 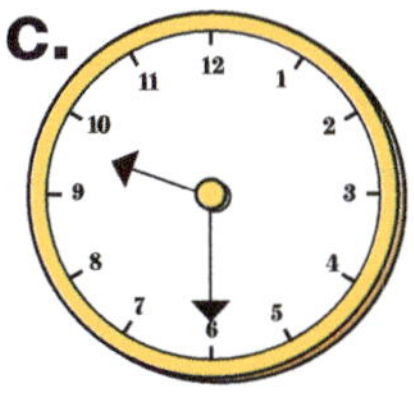

2. Write these times on the digital clocks.

a. Half past seven

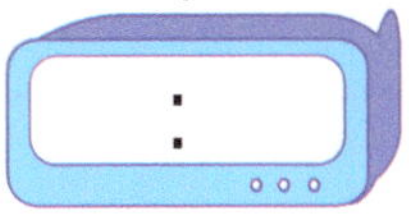

b. Eight o'clock

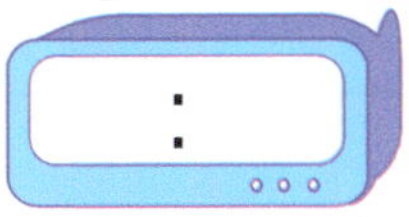

c. Six o'clock

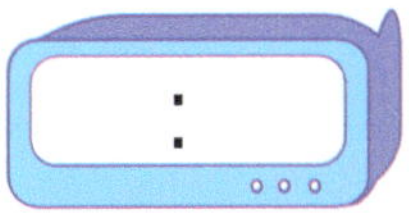

d. Nine thirty

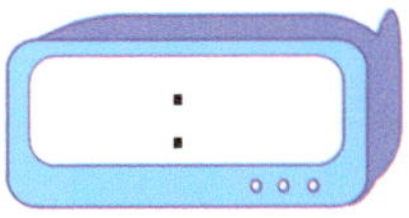

Addition

1. a. $7 + 5 =$ ☐ **b.** $9 + 6 =$ ☐

c. $8 + 4 =$ ☐ **d.** $7 + 8 =$ ☐

e. $9 + 6 =$ ☐ **f.** $12 + 5 =$ ☐

2. Add the numbers down the side to the top numbers.

+	9	3	2	7	6	11	12
7							
4							
8							

See the snake sliding by,
Watch the birds fly in the sky.
Hear the roos bounding along,
Their big back legs must be strong.

A platypus plays in a puddle,
Poor old wombat's in a muddle.
The kookaburra sits in his gum tree,
Here comes an emu running at me.

I'll now sit safely in the car.
Oh how special all animals are!
Australian animals are such fun,
LOOK! Over there, is another one!

Responding

Write words from the poem that rhyme with these words.

a. fly ____________ ____________

b. muddle ______________

c. strong ____________

d. tree ______________

e. car ____________

f. sun ____________ ____________

Interpreting

List the Australian animals named in the poem.

____________ ____________ ____________ ____________

____________ ____________ ____________

Sentences

Unjumble these words to write sentences or questions.

a. old How you are ______________________________?

b. like animals Australian I______________________________.

c. my koala's favourite are ______________________________.

d. you zoo Do visiting the like ______________________________?

e. get you Do cold ______________________________?

f. trees are Gum big very ______________________________.

Unit 4

Spelling

Look, cover, write, check each word.

word	write	check
snake	______	☐
along	______	☐
animals	______	☐
wombat	______	☐
koala	______	☐
special	______	☐
strong	______	☐
platypus	______	☐

Word Building

Add the missing **ow** sound to build the words.

ow

- sl __ __
- kn __ __
- sh __ __
- b __ __
- m __ __
- gr __ __
- fl __ __
- wind __ __
- bl __ __
- cr __ __

Opposites

Write the opposites for these words. Each opposite is in the frame.

night ______ high ______ bright ______ now ______

happy______ short______ back ______ yes ______

dull long low later day no front sad

Subtraction

1\.

a.	b.	c.	d.
16 - 8 = ___	12 -7 = ___	14 - 6 = ___	18 -13 = ___

e.	f.	g.	h.
17 - 11 = ___	20 - 14 = ___	13 - 5 = ___	19 - 6 = ___

2\. Darcy had 14 footy cards. He gave 6 to his little brother. How many does Darcy have left?

☐ - ☐ = ☐ cards

Fractions

1\. How many parts in each shape?

a.  ☐

b.  ☐

c.  ☐

d.  ☐

2\. How many parts are coloured?

a. 

$\frac{\square}{4}$

b. 

$\frac{\square}{8}$

c. 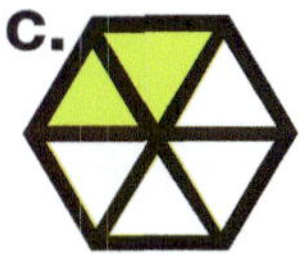

$\frac{\square}{6}$

My Dog Oscar

My dog is young and playful. His name is Oscar. He always wants to jump up and chase sticks and balls. He runs around all day long in the back yard.

He barks at the post lady. When he hears her bike coming, he runs to the gate waiting to see her. As soon as he sees her yellow jacket he starts barking. The postie just smiles and says: "Good dog, good dog!"

Sometimes, when I feed him he knocks his bowl over. Mum says you would think he hadn't been fed for a week. After he has gulped his food down he settles in front of the television. He likes the flicking of the screen. I love Oscar, he is a good pet.

Understanding

Colour the bubble that best fits each sentence ending.

a. Oscar my dog always

- ◯ lays around the yard.
- ◯ jumps and chases sticks.

b. He gets excited when he

- ◯ hears the post lady's bike.
- ◯ watching television.

c. Oscar knocks over his bowl

- ◯ sometimes
- ◯ always

d. How often is Oscar fed?

- ◯ once a week.
- ◯ every day.

Interpreting

Complete these sentences.

a. Oscar is playful and ______________________________

b. He starts to bark when ______________________________

Punctuation

Add capital letters, full stops or question marks when you rewrite these sentences.

a. i would like a pet dog, but i would name him rex

____

b. do dogs like oscar, that bark all day, scare you

____

Unit 5

Spelling

Look, cover, write, check each word.

word	write	check
young	____________	☐
jump	____________	☐
yard	____________	☐
waiting	____________	☐
smile	____________	☐
would	____________	☐
after	____________	☐
screen	____________	☐

Word Building

Add the missing **ar** sound to build the words.

ar

b__ __
f__ __
st__ __
b__ __k
m__ __k
sm __ __t
sh __ __k
d__ __k
st __ __t
c__ __d
t__ __
c__ __

Sentences

Write words from the family group above to complete these sentences.

a. Dad drove the __________ into the wet __________ in the __________.

b. There was a __________ in the letter box. It had a post __________.

c. The __________ in the __________ sky was the only bright light.

Mass

Order the mass of these objects 1-7 from **lightest** to **heaviest**.

☐ **a.** 

b.  ☐

c. 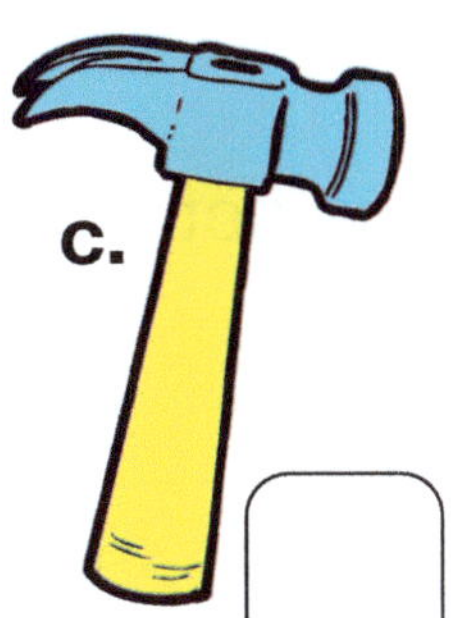 ☐

d.  ☐

e.  ☐

f.  ☐

g. 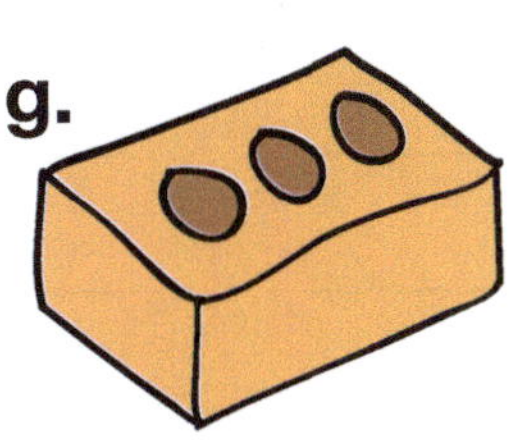 ☐

Groups

Count how many in each group, then write the number sentence.

a.

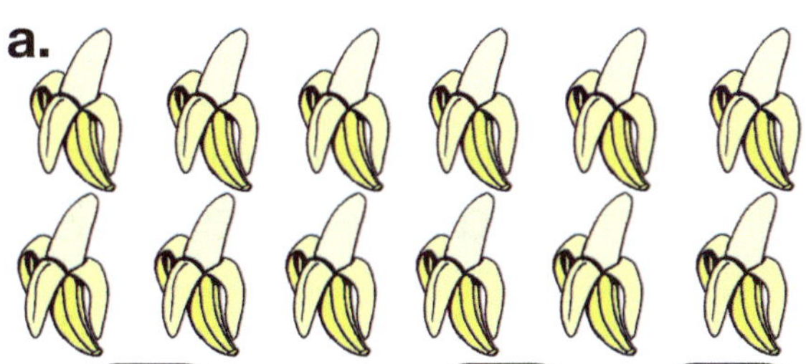

= ☐

= ☐

☐ groups of ☐ = ☐

b.

= ☐

= ☐

= ☐

☐ groups of ☐ = ☐

Monster School Fete

Come One! to Come All!

Gully Lane School Monster Fete

Saturday 6th April, 10am till 4pm

Attractions:

Jumping Castle	Hoopla	Hot Dogs and Pies
Toffee Stall	Face Painting	Pets on Parade
Pony Rides	Knock'em Down	Tea and Coffee
Book Sale	Uniform Sale	Super Herbert the magician
Sausage Sizzle	Lucky dips	

All money raised will buy new computers for Year 2 classes

Understanding Colour the bubble that best fits the poster information.

a. The school fete is on
- ◯ a school day.
- ◯ Saturday.

b. Attractions at the fete include
- ◯ Pony rides.
- ◯ Merry go round.

c. The word monster fete means
- ◯ scary
- ◯ big

d. Is Super Herbert a
- ◯ super hero
- ◯ magician

Interpreting List who would enjoy these activities under the headings: Adults, Children, Both.

Jumping Castle   Toffee Stall   Pony Rides   Book Sale   Sausage Sizzle
Hoopla   Face Painting   Knock'em Down   Uniform Sale   Lucky dips
Hot Dogs and Pies   Pets on Parade   Tea and Coffee
Super Herbert the magician

Adults	Children	Both
____________	____________	____________
____________	____________	____________
____________	____________	____________
____________	____________	____________

Unit 6

Spelling

Look, cover, write, check each word.

word	write	check
castle	______	☐
lucky	______	☐
stall	______	☐
uniform	______	☐
monster	______	☐
April	______	☐
down	______	☐
sausage	______	☐

Word Families

Add the missing **ea** to build word families.

ea

s __ __ t
m __ __ t
p __ __ ch
r __ __ d
b __ __ ds
sl __ __ t
tr __ __ t
cr __ __ m
st __ __ k
sp __ __ k

Sentences

Unjumble the words to write sentences.

a. are to going My Monster family the Saturday. on Fete

____

b. sizzle cooking Dad sausage is the BBQ. a on

____

c. will fete. on Ride go I a Pony the at

____

Money

1. Name the coins.

a.  ______________

b.  ______________

c.  ______________

2. What is the value of these coins?

Lines

Match the lines to their names.

a. 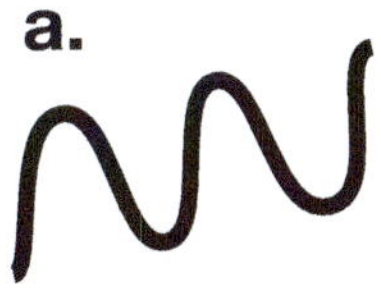

b. 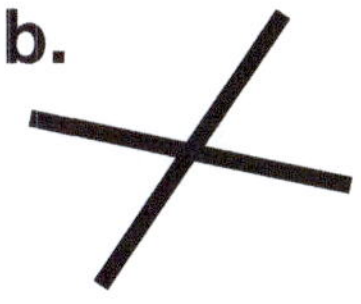

c. 

d. 

e.

f. 

horizontal line

crossed lines

curved lines

broken line

parallel lines

zig zag line

My Birthday Party

On Saturday I am having a birthday party. I am eight. I have invited my school friends and my soccer team mates. Mum has been shopping buying all the food, lollies, chips, hats and drinks for the party. She went to see Mrs Jones next door, to ask her to make a birthday cake for the party. It will have eight candles.

Dad has cleaned up the back yard and mowed the lawn. He is setting up all the games. I am helping him.

We will have lots of fun games and food to eat. My friends will have a good time at my party. I am excited. I can't wait for Saturday.

Understanding Colour the bubble that best fits each question or sentence.

a. The party is to celebrate
- ◯ the soccer team.
- ◯ my school friends.
- ◯ my birthday.

b. Mum went shopping
- ◯ to buy a birthday cake.
- ◯ to buy party foods.
- ◯ to see Mrs Jones.

c. Dad and I set up
- ◯ the back yard
- ◯ my bedroom
- ◯ the fun games

d. Why will there be eight candles?
- ◯ Eight is my favourite number.
- ◯ I am turning eight.
- ◯ There will be eight friends.

Responding Complete these sentences.

a. The birthday party is for an eight year old on ____________________.

b. My friends from ____________ and the ____________ ____________ will come.

c. There will be lots of ____________ and ____________ at the ____________.

Writing Write a short story about a birthday party.

____

____

____

____

Unit 7

Spelling

Look, cover, write, check each word.

word	write	check
school		
friend		
drink		
party		
clean		
yard		
lawn		
next		

Word Building

Add the missing **ing** to build word families.

ing

sw__ __ __

d__ __ __

k__ __ __

w__ __ __

br__ __ __

cl__ __ __

p__ __ __

st__ __ __

r__ __ __

th__ __ __

cl__ __ __

s__ __ __

People Who Help Us

Label the people who help us. Use the word bank.

a. 

b. 

c. 

d. 

e. 

f. 

Word Bank

- Police Officer
- Doctor
- Fireman
- Paramedic
- Nurse
- Teacher

Addition

1.

a.

	tens	ones
	7	2
+	2	6

b.

	tens	ones
	3	4
+	2	3

c.

	tens	ones
	5	4
+	1	5

2. A boy saved $23 in one month. He was given another $44 for his birthday. How much does he have in total? Write the algorithm.

	tens	ones
$		
+$		
$		

Area

Count the squares in each shape.
Colour the **biggest** area yellow and the **smallest** red.

a. 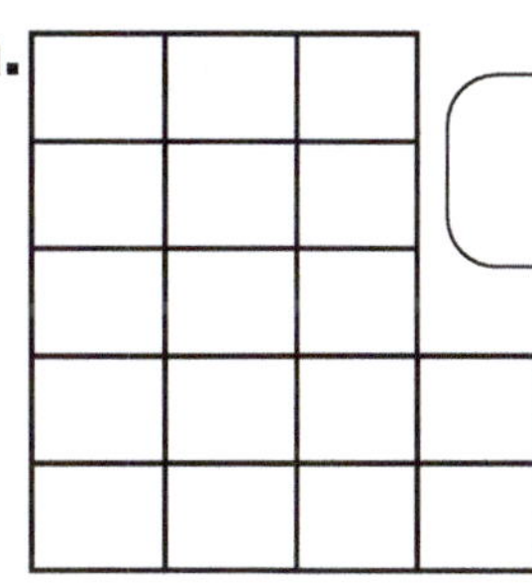

b. 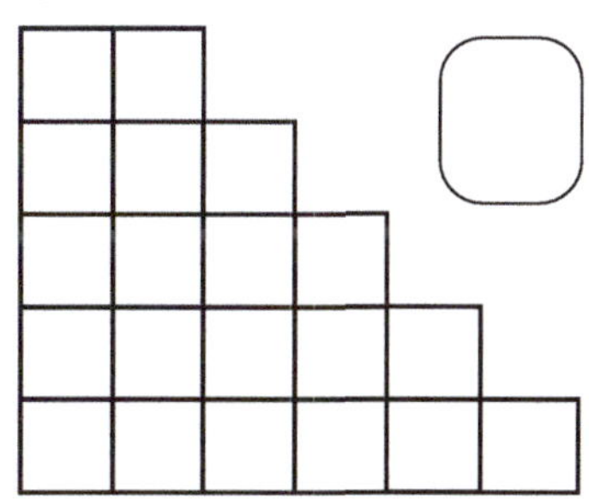

c. 

Post Card to Grandma

Dear Grandma,
Simon and I are having a good time here in Queensland. We went to the Theme Park yesterday. Simon and I sat in the front seat on the Big Dipper. It was scary because we were going fast. All the people behind us were yelling and screaming.
Today we are going to the mall with mum and aunt Nesha, then to the water slide.

Love Ellie

Mrs M. Holmes
75 Alley Street
Belltown
NSW 2222

Understanding Colour the bubble that best fits each sentence.

a. Simon and Ellie are
- ◯ brother and sister.
- ◯ cousins.
- ◯ only friends.

b. The big Dipper is
- ◯ at the Water Slide
- ◯ at the Theme Park
- ◯ in New South Wales

c. Grandma's name is
- ◯ Mrs Holmes
- ◯ Ellie
- ◯ the mother of Nesha

d. A post card is like
- ◯ a parcel
- ◯ a phone call
- ◯ a letter

Interpreting Complete these sentences.

a. Grandma lives in the town of ____________________.

b. Her state and post code are ________________________.

Punctuation Rewrite these sentences adding capital letters, full stops or question marks.

a. my name is ellie

____

b. my grandma is mrs holmes

____

c. do you go on holidays to queensland

____

Unit 8

Spelling

Look, cover, write, check each word.

word	write	check
people		
with		
went		
yesterday		
tomorrow		
water		
slide		
fast		

Word Building

Add the missing **er** to build a word family.

er

sist __ __

moth__ __

pap __ __

summ__ __

ti __ __

wint __ __

f__ __n

fath__ __

flow __ __

lett __ __

broth__ __

Opposites

Write the opposites of these words.

in ____	fast ____	new ____	down ____
good ____	last ____	first ____	small ____
front ____	wild ____	day ____	happy ____

Patterns

1. Complete each pattern.

a.	2	4		8	10			16
b.	6		12	15		21	24	
c.	10	15	20		30	35		

2. Write the totals.

a. $9 + 6 =$ ☐ **b.** $7 + 5 =$ ☐

c. $8 + 12 =$ ☐ **d.** $15 + 3 =$ ☐

e. $11 + 2 =$ ☐ **f.** $21 + 5 =$ ☐

Time

Draw a line to match times that are the same.

a. 6 : 15

b. 2 : 45

c. 4 : 45

d. 8 : 30

A.
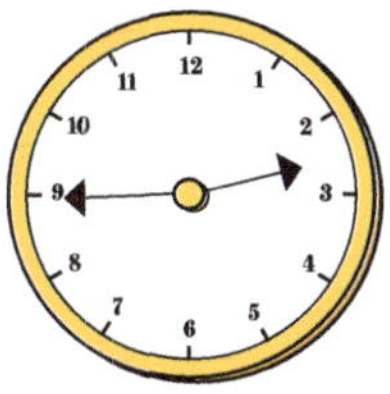

B.
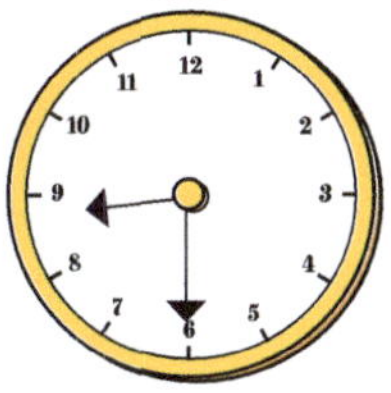

C.
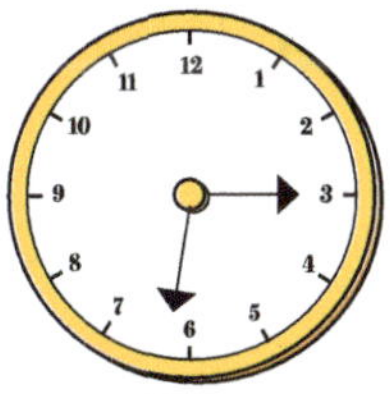

D.

Go-Karting

Last Saturday, I went go-karting with my friend William Abbot, at the Show Ground. It has a new Go-kart track there. The track was busy with lots of teenagers pushing each other while they waited their turn. The man selling the tickets said we were "juniors" so he gave us a discount.

William and I raced around the track. I hit the tyres on the wall a couple of times but still beat William the first time. We raced three more times. William won all those races, but it didn't matter, we had a good time.

On the way home we ate a pie. It was yummy.

Understanding Colour the bubble that best fits each sentence.

a. We went go-karting
- ◯ at the Show Ground.
- ◯ last Friday.
- ◯ in our go-karts.

b. There were lots of
- ◯ busy ticket sellers.
- ◯ teenagers pushing each other.
- ◯ go-kart tracks.

c. Juniors at the go-kart track
- ◯ don't wear safety gear.
- ◯ get a discount.
- ◯ wait till teenagers finish.

d. William and I had
- ◯ one race.
- ◯ three races.
- ◯ four races.

Interpreting Complete each sentence.

a. William and I are ______________________________.

b. We ate our pies on ______________________________.

Grammar Adverbs tell more about how something is done. Choose an adverb to add to these sentences.

a. William drove very ______________ to beat me.

b. I always eat my pie ______________ because they are hot.

c. We walked ______________ to the ticket office.

d. The teenagers waited ______________ until their turn.

Adverbs
quickly
fast
noisily
carefully

Spelling

Look, cover, write, check each word.

word	write	check
each	______	☐
waited	______	☐
around	______	☐
first	______	☐
those	______	☐
great	______	☐
ticket	______	☐
junior	______	☐

Word Families

Add the missing **or** to build words.

or

- c __ __ k
- c __ __ d
- c __ __ n
- f __ __ t
- st __ __ k
- expl __ __ er
- f __ __ ce
- p __ __ k
- h __ __ se
- f __ __ k

Sentences

Draw a line to match sentence beginning and endings.

a. I went go-karting	tickets for four races.
b. We were given	we ate a pie.
c. The teenagers were	with my friend William.
d. On the way home	waiting to buy tickets.

Flip, Slide, Turn

Colour the action card describing the movement of those shapes.

a. 

slid along
flipped over
turned around

b. 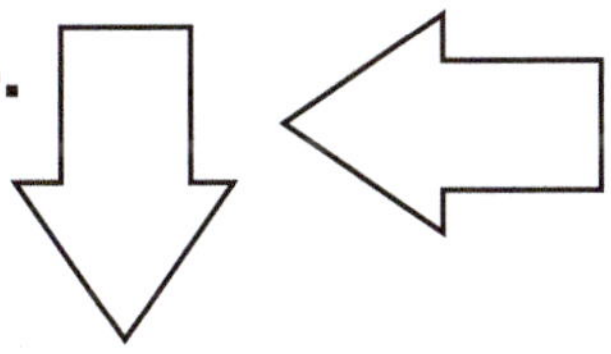

slid along
flipped over
turned around

c. 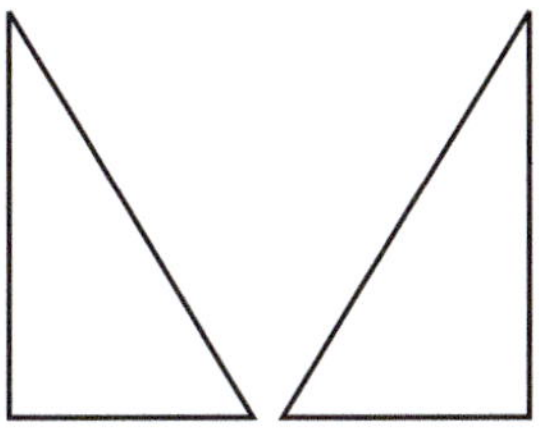

slid along
flipped over
turned around

Money

Colour the notes, then count the amount of money in each group.

a. 

= $ ☐

b. 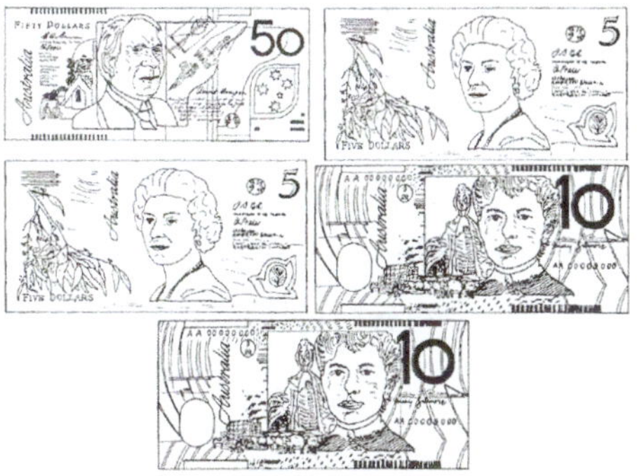

= $ ☐

The Moon Legend

In the Dreamtime, a small moon left the valley of the moons to cross the sky. The moon travelled in the night sky and sometimes in the daytime near the sun.

Soon it grew to be a full moon but the sun didn't like it, so it chased the moon across the sky, tearing pieces off it until it was gone. The pieces that broke off become stars.

Since that time, each month a new moon leaves the valley of the moons, grows to a full moon but then is chased and destroyed by the sun.

---

a. Tick the word that describes how the sun felt about the moon.

☐ friendly ☐ happy ☐ angry

b. Is this legend true? ☐ yes ☐ no

c. How many days does a moon live each month? ☐

d. How many full moons are there in a year? ☐

Grammar

Remember verbs are "doing" or "action" words. They are used as commands. Use each of these action verbs as a command.

Get Stop Ask Spread Cut

a. ___ ___ ___ ___ that boy from running in the hall.

b. ___ ___ ___ the new girl to sit near Emma.

c. ___ ___ ___ ___ ___ ___ the news that we won the finals.

d. ___ ___ ___ William, Simon and Amed to help you.

e. ___ ___ ___ the grass across the front of the house.

Punctuation

Add capitals and full stops, when rewriting each sentence.

today is wednesday and jon is going to luna park

____

paris and alex went to see their grand parents in perth

____

Spelling

Look, cover, write, check each word.

word	write	check
small	________________	☐
cross	________________	☐
travel	________________	☐
become	________________	☐
since	________________	☐
chase	________________	☐
sometimes	________________	☐
leave	________________	☐

Word Families

Add **ed** to build words in the past tense.

ed

wash __ __
talk __ __
hand __ __
walk __ __
bark __ __
yell __ __
laugh __ __
cheer __ __
lock __ __
rain __ __
roll __ __

Sentences

Unjumble these sentences.

a. and legends tell Myths stories. time old

____

b. like grandma. visit my I to Melbourne in

____

Mass

Colour the correct arrow to show what happens when the cat on the right gets off the beam.

a.

b.

Time

Show these times on each clock face.

a. 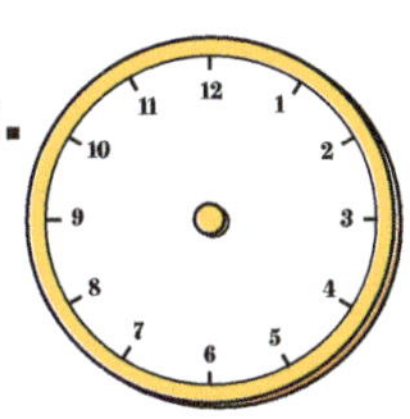
half past nine

b. 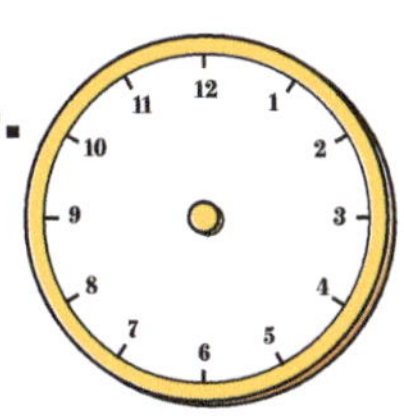
quarter past five

c. 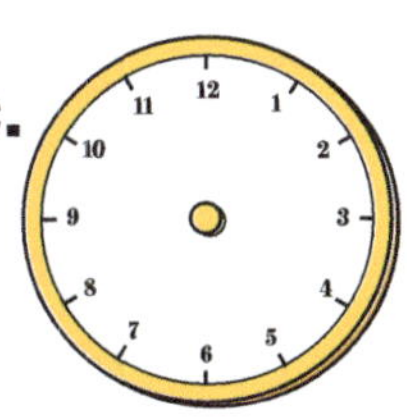
quarter to eleven

d. 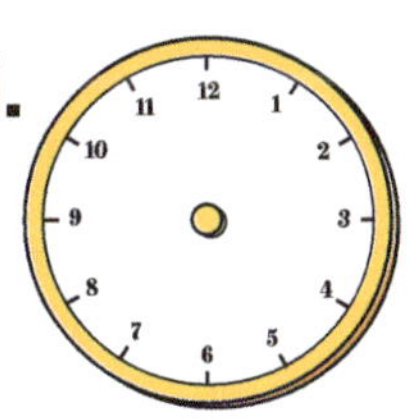
quarter to five

e. 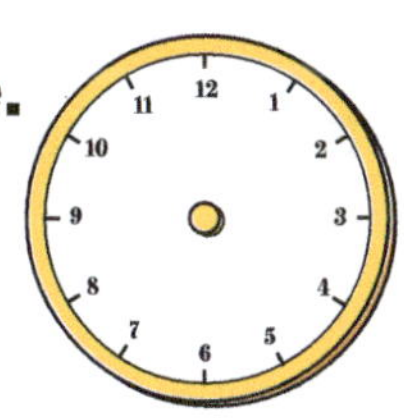
quarter past six

f. 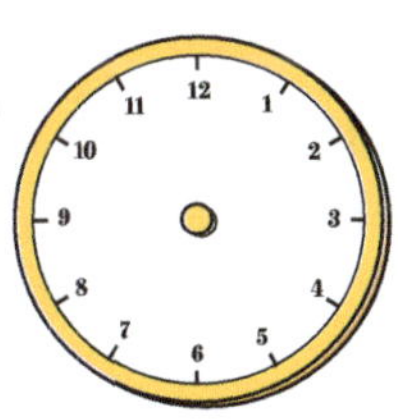
nine o'clock

Our Environment - Poem

Don't throw all your rubbish away.
Try and use it in another way.
Bottles, paper and cans we must recycle.
To save our environment, this is vital.
Do your bit and wear a grin.
Put all your rubbish in the bin.
Help save the environment for us all
So trees and people can grow tall.

Responding

Write words that rhyme with these words.

a. bin ____________ ____________ ____________

b. way ____________ ____________ ____________

c. all ____________ ____________ ____________

d. glass ____________ ____________ ____________

Meanings

Match the words from the poem with the correct meanings.

a. rubbish — the world around us

b. recycle — keep things safe or the same

c. environment — a big smile

d. vital — use again

e. save — waste material

f. grin — very important

Writing

Write an acrostic using the word RECYCLE.

R ____________

E ____________

C ____________

Y ____________

C ____________

L ____________

E ____________

Sentences

Unjumble these sentences.

a. tree green. Plant Australia make and a

____

b. and paper save Recycle tree. a help

____

Unit 11

Spelling

Look, cover, write, check each word.

word	write	check
throw	______________	☐
another	______________	☐
recycle	______________	☐
rubbish	______________	☐
bottle	______________	☐
paper	______________	☐
important	______________	☐
material	______________	☐

Word Building

Add **ai** to build word families.

ai

n__ __l

p__ __nt

br__ __n

dr__ __n

g__ __n

gr__ __n

tr__ __n

sn__ __l

s__ __l

p__ __n

r__ __n

Pollution

Draw an **x** in the box on things that cause polution and tick ✓ those that are good for our environment.

a.  ☐

b.  ☐

c. 

☐

d.  ☐

e. 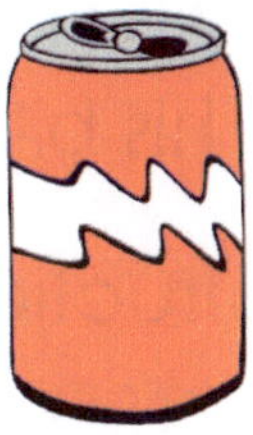 ☐

f.  ☐

Capacity

1. Colour the containers that will **NOT** hold water.

a. 

b. 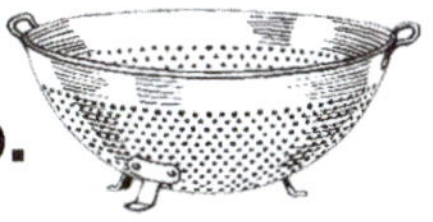

c. 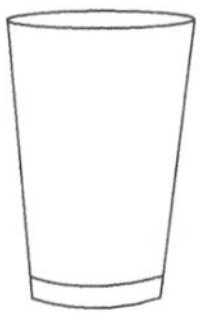

d. 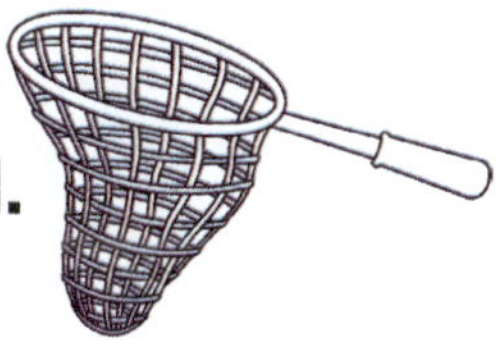

e. 

f. 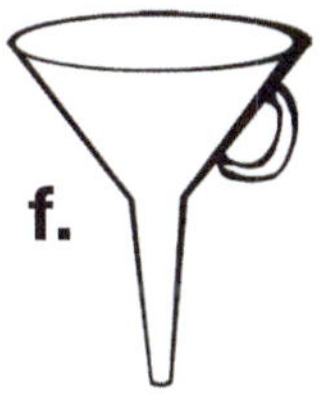

2. Colour the container that will hold the most.

Subtraction

1. Try these vertical subtractions.

a. $\begin{array}{r} 9 \\ -4 \\ \hline \end{array}$ b. $\begin{array}{r} 7 \\ -3 \\ \hline \end{array}$ c. $\begin{array}{r} 8 \\ -6 \\ \hline \end{array}$ d. $\begin{array}{r} 10 \\ -1 \\ \hline \end{array}$

2. Take the number around the circle from the middle number.

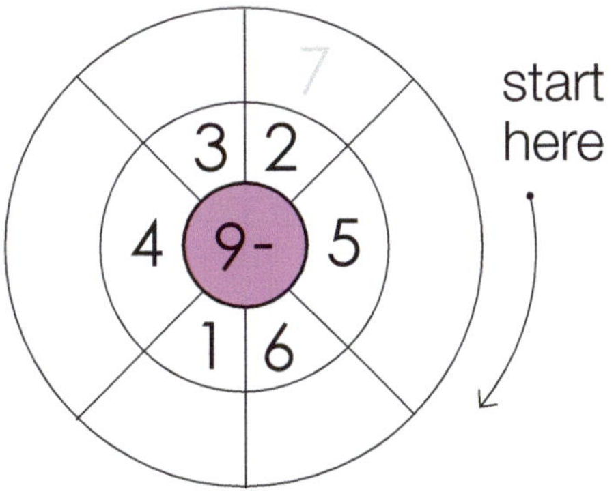

Raining

"Oh! It is still raining. How long must it go on?" I complained. Mum looked at me with a frown and said: "It's only been raining since Saturday afternoon. It will stop soon."

"How do you know that mum? I want to go out and ride my bike in the park." I explained.

Well, you'll just have to wait until it stops or if you want to get wet, make sure you wear a coat, your helmet and shoes."

"Really!" I exclaimed, "Can I ride in the rain?"

"Yes, but take Simon with you. He would enjoy that too!" she said.

"OK. Simon, get your coat, helmet and boots. We are riding our bikes in the park. Hurry up." I yelled.

Understanding

Colour the bubble that best fits each sentence or question.

a. What did the author want to do?

- ◯ ride in the rain.
- ◯ complain to his mother.
- ◯ ride his bike in the park.

b. What did mum reply?

- ◯ the rain would stop soon.
- ◯ wear a coat, helmet and shoes.
- ◯ wait till it stopped raining.

c. What instruction did Simon get?

- ◯ hurry up!
- ◯ wait till the rain stops.
- ◯ come and talk to mum.

d. If they went riding in the park?

- ◯ They would go fast.
- ◯ They would get wet.
- ◯ They would not need helmets.

Interpreting

a. Who will enjoy riding in the rain too? ______________________________

b. When did the rain start to fall? ______________________________

c. Where were the boys going to ride their bikes? ______________________________

Punctuation

Inverted commas or speech bubbles are used to show someone is speaking. Add inverted commas to these sentences. (" ")

a. I think it is going to rain, tomorrow. said William.

b. Will you take me to the shops to buy new shoes? asked Ali.

c. Tell me more about the new bike. said grandma.

d. Hurray, hurray, I think we won lotto, yelled mum.

Unit 12 Spelling

Look, cover, write, check each word.

word	write	check
said	______	☐
since	______	☐
know	______	☐
bicycle	______	☐
coat	______	☐
enjoy	______	☐
park	______	☐
would	______	☐

Word Building

Add **ake** to build word families.
Note the **'a'** is pronounced as **'A'**.

ake

m___ t___ sn___ l___ fl___ sh___ w___ b___ r___ c___

Sentences

Complete answers to these questions.

How old are you? I am ______________________

Do you have a dog? Yes I ______________________

What is your teacher's name? My teacher's name is ______________________

Place Value

1. Write the number shown on each place value card.

a. 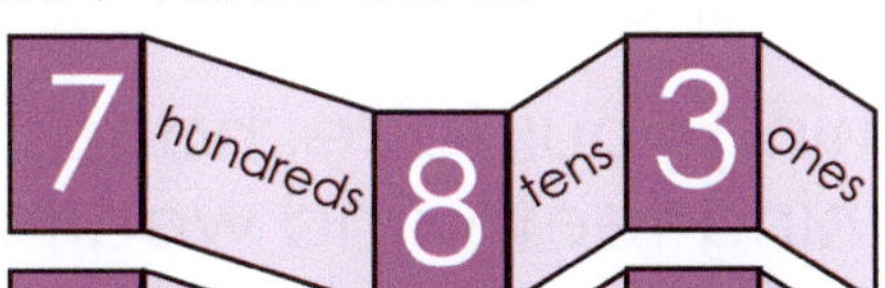

______

b. 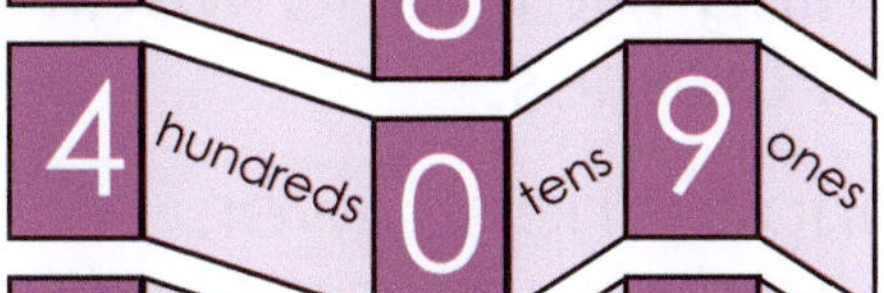

______

c. 

______

2. Write the number shown on each abacus.

a. 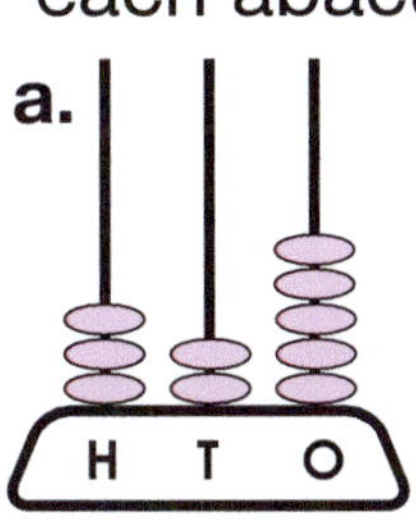

______

b. 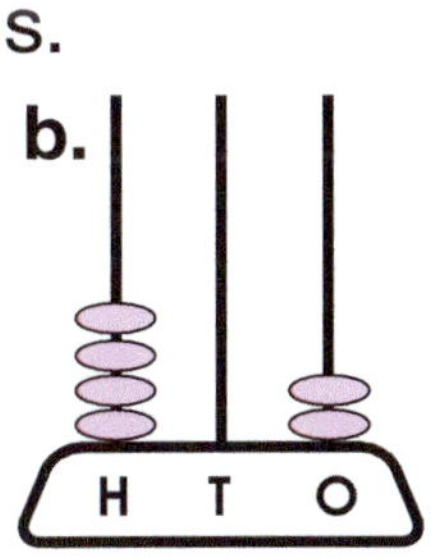

______

c. 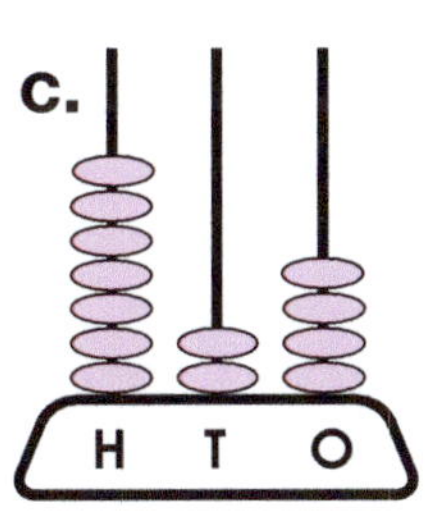

______

Addition

1. Complete each addition algorithm.

a.

	H	T	O
	3	2	4
+	1	5	5

b.

	H	T	O
	6	2	1
+	1	3	7

c.

	H	T	O
	8	3	3
+		2	6

d.

	H	T	O
	4	3	6
+	4	1	2

e.

	H	T	O
	3	3	3
+	2	4	6

f.

	H	T	O
	1	7	8
+	3	2	0

2. Simon had $138 in his bank. Grandma gave him $60 for his birthday. How much does he have now?

$ ______________________

Stay Clean

Why do we need to stay clean? Keeping your body clean by washing yourself daily in a shower or a bath will help keep you clean and also help stop you from getting sick.

Mum usually washes your clothes so you don't smell. The smell comes from bacteria (back-tear-ee-ah) on your skin or in your clothes. It is bacteria that makes you sick.

When you wash your hands most bacteria is washed away. When mum washes your clothes, bacteria is removed and clothes have that nice fresh, clean smell.

It is very important to wash your hands after going to the toilet and before you eat. You get rid of any bacteria when you do that. This will help you from getting sick. Remember always wash your face and hands, clean your teeth and wear clean clothes to stay fresh and clean.

Understanding

Colour the bubble that best fits each sentence or question.

a. Why is back-tear-ee-ah put in brackets the first time?

- ◯ To show how it is spelt.
- ◯ To show how to say it.
- ◯ To show what it means.

b. What is it that makes you sick?

- ◯ Your teacher.
- ◯ Having to do homework.
- ◯ Bacteria.

c. How does mum help get rid of bacteria?

- ◯ By washing our clothes.
- ◯ Going shopping.
- ◯ Helping you have a bath.

d. How can you stay fresh?

- ◯ By washing hands only.
- ◯ Washing your face, hands, cleaning teeth and wearing clean clothes.
- ◯ Staying in the shower.

Interpreting

Write an ending for each sentence.

a. You can avoid getting sick by ______________________________

b. Bacteria can be found ______________________________

c. You should stay fresh and clean ______________________________

d. Washing your clothes helps stop ______________________________

Unit 13

Spelling

Look, cover, write, check each word.

word	write	check
clean	____________	☐
daily	____________	☐
clothes	____________	☐
remove	____________	☐
fresh	____________	☐
bacteria	____________	☐
before	____________	☐
yourself	____________	☐

Word Building

Add **ck** to build word families.

ck

du__ __

bri__ __

sti__ __

clo__ __

sa__ __

so__ __

si__ __

cli__ __

stu__ __

sta__ __

ro__ __et

bu__ __et

po__ __et

Spelling

Use list words or **ck** words to complete each sentence.

a. Uri had a handful of marbles in his ______________________ .

b. The best way to ______________ bacteria is to was regularly.

c. I have a shower ______________ to keep fresh and clean.

d. Always keep ______________ clean to stop from getting ____________ .

Area

Count the squares in each shape.

a.

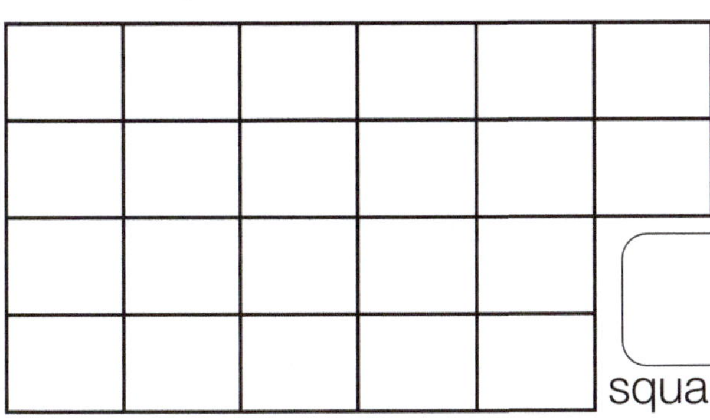

☐ squares

b.

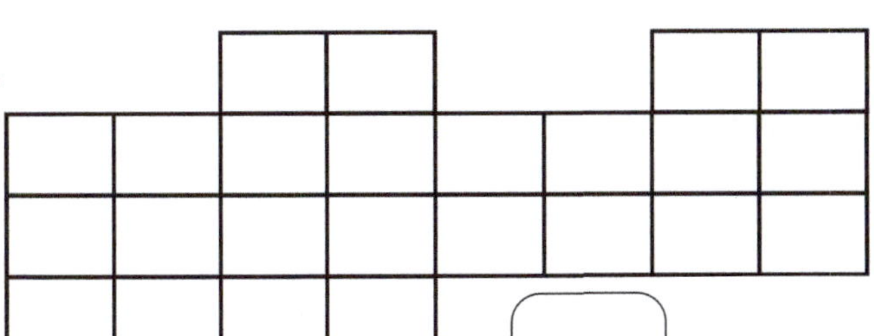

☐ squares

More Money

Add value of notes and coins in each group.

a.

= $ ______

b.

= $ ______

c.

= $ ______

The Four Seasons

There are four seasons every year - summer, autumn, winter and spring.

Seasons happen because the earth tilts on its axis as it orbits around the sun.
When it is winter in the southern hemisphere, it is summer in the northern hemisphere. The southern hemisphere is further away from the sun. This results in less heat reaching the southern hemisphere in winter. Six months later, when the earth's axis is tilted the other way, it is winter in the northern hemisphere and summer in the southern hemisphere.

The changes in season affect the way we dress, the foods we eat, the games we play and the energy we use.

Response

Write a response to these.

a. In which hemisphere do we live? ______________________

b. If it is summer here what season is it in the other hemisphere? ______________________

c. What season comes before spring? ______________________

Our Seasons

List some of the foods we eat in these seasons.

Winter	Spring	Summer
____________	____________	____________
____________	____________	____________
____________	____________	____________
____________	____________	____________

Opposites

The opposite of **day** is **night**.
Write the opposite of these words.

a. summer ______________

b. high ______________

c. bottom ______________

d. hot ______________

e. open ______________

f. large ______________

g. north ______________

Plurals

Words are made plural (more than one) by adding **s**. Write these words as plurals.

hat ____________ dog ____________

chair ____________ year ____________

month ____________ cat ____________

season ____________ day ____________

lizard ____________ boy ____________

Unit 14

Spelling

Look, cover, write, check each word.

word	write	check
season	______	☐
summer	______	☐
autumn	______	☐
south	______	☐
further	______	☐
months	______	☐
change	______	☐
energy	______	☐

Word Building

Add **ir** to build word families.

ir

- th__ __d
- g__ __l
- d__ __t
- th__ __st
- th__ __ty
- squ__ __t
- sh __ __t
- b__ __thday
- c__ __cus
- f__ __st
- sk__ __t
- b__ __d

Groupings

Write one word for each group of words. One is done for you.

cat, dog, horse, cow *animals*

a. blue, green, red, yellow ______

b. May, July, June ______

c. summer, winter, spring ______

d. baby, boy, girl ______

e. apple, pear, banana ______

f. cricket, tennis, football ______

Subtraction

Regroup tens for ones, then continue the subtraction. One is done.

	T	O
	5	13
	~~6~~	~~3~~
-	2	5
	3	8

a.

	T	O
	3	2
-	1	9

b.

	T	O
	6	5
-	3	7

c.

	T	O
	8	1
-	2	6

d.

	T	O
	4	4
-	2	8

e.

	T	O
	6	0
-	3	2

Fractions

Tick the fraction coloured in each shape.

a.  $\frac{1}{2}$ ☐ $\frac{1}{4}$ ☐ $\frac{1}{3}$ ☐

b. 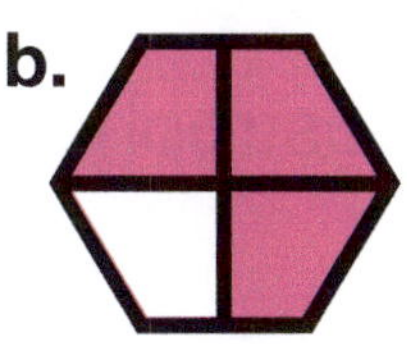 $\frac{1}{2}$ ☐ $\frac{1}{4}$ ☐ $\frac{3}{4}$ ☐

c. 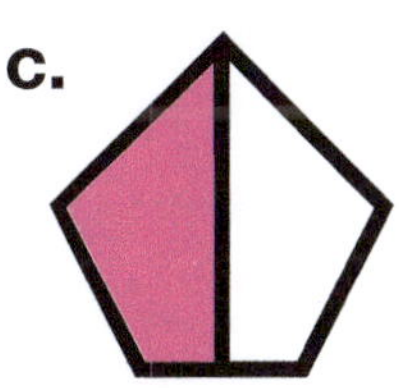 $\frac{1}{2}$ ☐ $\frac{1}{4}$ ☐ $\frac{1}{8}$ ☐

d.  $\frac{1}{2}$ ☐ $\frac{1}{4}$ ☐ $\frac{1}{8}$ ☐

Keep the Environment Clean

It is important to keep our waterways clean because water is vital for every living thing. The water we drink in cities and towns is cleaned before it comes out of the tap. If the environment is not kept clean, some of the run-off water can become polluted. This may cause damage to the environment, so we must all make an effort to keep our waterways clean.

In other countries where water is not cleaned before drinking and the water-ways are very polluted, people often get sick. Sometimes animals drink polluted water and get sick. When people eat meat or drink milk from these animals they can get sick too!

Clean, fresh water is vital for our community, animals and environment. Help keep our environment clean and safe for us and the future.

Understanding

Colour the bubble that best fits each sentence.

a. What happens to city water before it comes from the tap?

- ◯ it is shared with animals.
- ◯ it is cleaned.
- ◯ it is straight from the dams.

b. Contaminated food can be caused by:

- ◯ polluted water.
- ◯ water run-off.
- ◯ damaged environment.

Interpreting

Complete each sentence.

a. Polluted water may cause ____________________

b. Our community depends on ____________________

Abbreviations

Shorten these by using an apostrophe.

he will ________ she is ________

has not ________ we are ________

is not ________ do not ________

have not ________ I will ________

she will ________

Plurals

Some words need **es** to make plural. Write these words as plurals.

bus ________ class ________

dress ________ fox ________

church ________ box ________

match ________ wish ________

dish ________ fix ________

Unit 15 Spelling

Look, cover, write, check each word.

word	write	check
become	____________	☐
water	____________	☐
drink	____________	☐
effort	____________	☐
animal	____________	☐
people	____________	☐
future	____________	☐
cause	____________	☐

Word Building

Add **ou** to build word families.

ou

- h __ __ se
- __ __ t
- ab __ __ t
- sh __ __ t
- h __ __ nd
- r __ __ nd
- pr __ __ d
- s __ __ nd
- c __ __ ud
- l __ __ d
- __ __ r
- m __ __ se

Sentences

Draw a line from sentence beginnings to a matching end.

a. Water is vital for	can become polluted.
b. Water run off	before it comes out of the tap.
c. People can get sick	every day living.
d. City water is cleaned	by drinking polluted water.

Length

Measure these using a ruler.

a.

☐ cm

b.

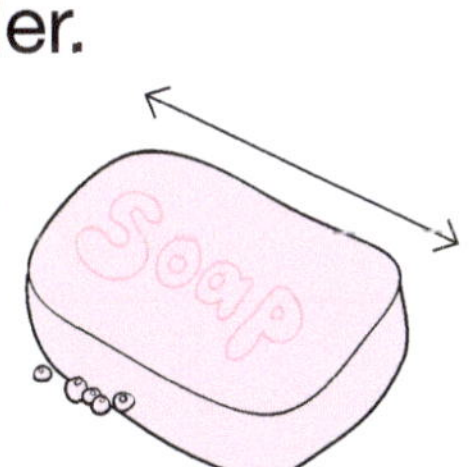

☐ cm

c.

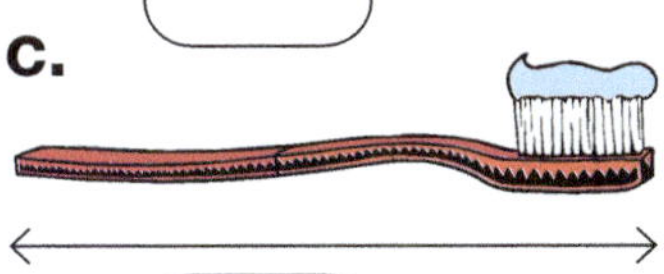

☐ cm

d.

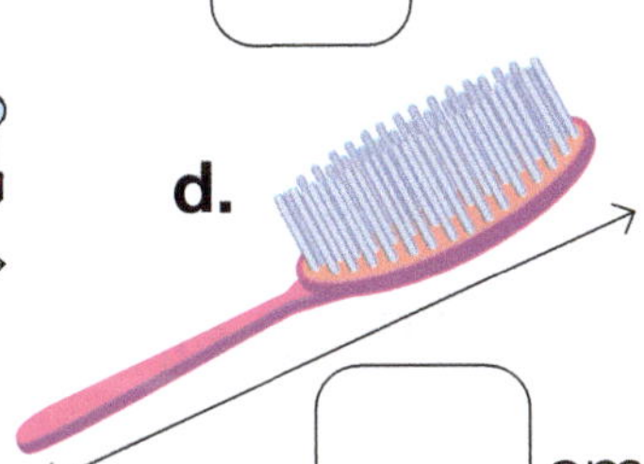

☐ cm

e.

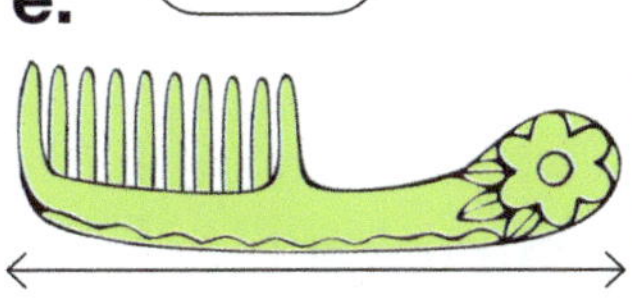

☐ cm

f.

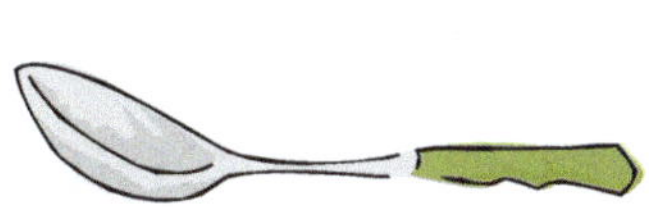

☐ cm

Corners and Edges

1. Count corners and edges on each shape.

a.

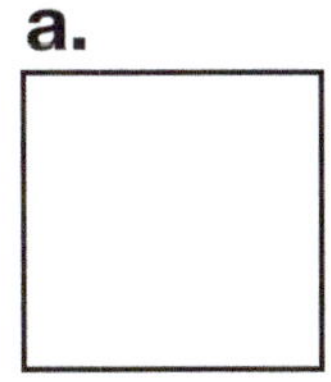

☐ corners
☐ edges

b.

☐ corners
☐ edges

c.

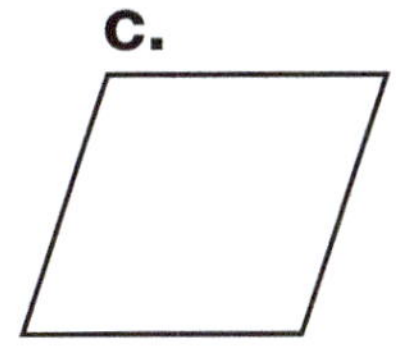

☐ corners
☐ edges

d.

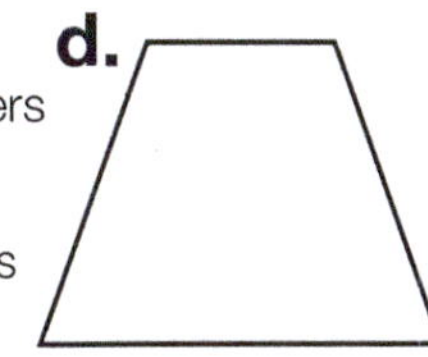

☐ corners
☐ edges

2. Do all four sided shapes have 4 corners? ____________

All 4 sided and 4 edged shapes are called quadrilaterals.
Quad means 4, tri means 3.

Mum's Having a Baby

Yesterday, when Erin arrived home from school, dad told her mum had gone to Canberra Hospital. She had pains and the Dr Fuller called an ambulance.

"Has she had the baby yet? Can we go and see her in hospital this afternoon?" asked Erin.

"No, the baby hasn't arrived yet." answered dad. "We will go and see her before tea, then on the way home we can get some take away." he explained.

"At what time will we leave?" asked Erin.

"As soon as Kate gets off the bus. It arrives about four o'clock." he said. Kate goes to Barton High School.

"Don't worry Erin." said dad. "Mum and the baby will be fine."

Understanding

Colour the bubble that best fits each sentence.

a. How did mum go to hospital?

- ◯ with the doctor
- ◯ dad took her
- ◯ by ambulance

b. When was the family visiting mum?

- ◯ after tea
- ◯ after four o'clock
- ◯ when the baby arrived

Responding

Complete each sentence.

a. Mum went to hospital ______________________________

b. Erin and dad had to wait ______________________________

c. On the way home dad and the girls ______________________________

Punctuation

Add capital letters, full stops or question marks to these sentences.

a. ☐ad and ☐rin waited for ☐ate to arrive home ◯

b. ☐he doctor's name was ☐r ☐uller

c. ☐as dad thinking about ☐rin and ☐ate's dinner ☐

d. ☐ate went to ☐arton ☐igh ☐chool in ☐anberra ◯

Unit 16

Spelling

Look, cover, write, check each word.

word	write	check
arrived	____________	☐
hospital	____________	☐
doctor	____________	☐
ambulance	____________	☐
answer	____________	☐
explain	____________	☐
leave	____________	☐
worry	____________	☐

Word Building

Add **ate** to build word families.

ate

- l__ __ __
- d__ __ __
- m__ __ __
- g__ __ __
- pl__ __ __
- r__ __ __
- cre__ __ __
- st__ __ __
- sl__ __ __

Our Community

Match each sign and symbol with its label.

CHILDREN CROSSING | WHEEL CHAIR ONLY | RESTAURANT | NO SMOKING

INFORMATION CENTRE | CAR PARK | AIRPORT | SPEED LIMIT

Number

Write the missing number in each row.

						missing number
a.	6	8	10	14	16	
b.	50	55	65	70	75	80	
c.	24	22	20	16	14	12	
d.	100	90	80	60	50	40	

2D Shapes

Draw the shape you will see when each is **flipped** to the **left**.

a.

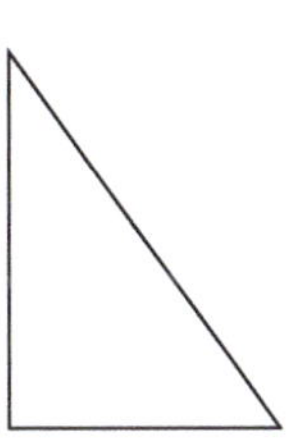

b.

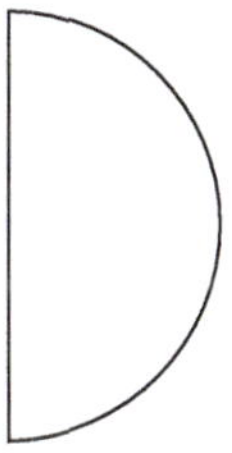

c.

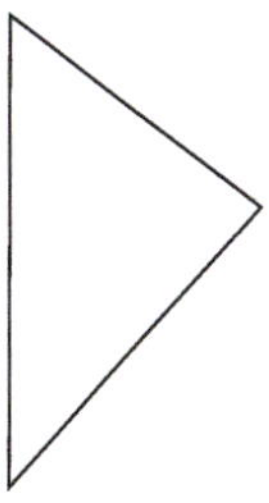

d.

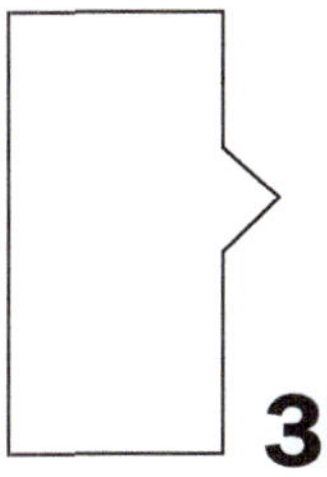

The Emu

Last weekend we went to the zoo to see the animals. One that sticks in my mind is the emu. It is Australia's biggest bird that doesn't fly. We were told that it can run very fast with its long skinny legs.

The eggs emus lay are green and the male emu sits on the eggs till they hatch. With most other feathered animals, the female sits on the eggs till they hatch. When the eggs hatch, the male emu looks after the little chicks. He gathers the food for the chicks. He is very caring just like my dad, who looks after mum and us. I like emus.

Understanding

Tick the box next to information you find in the text.

a. ☐ Emus love to fly.
b. ☐ Emus are Australian animals.
c. ☐ Emu eggs are green.
d. ☐ All emus live in zoos.
e. ☐ Male emus sit on eggs.
f. ☐ Male emus are caring.
g. ☐ Female emus gather food.
h. ☐ The author's dad is caring too.

Interpreting

Colour the bubble that best fits these questions or sentences.

a. We went to the zoo
- ◯ last Saturday.
- ◯ last Sunday
- ◯ last weekend.

b. With other feathered animals
- ◯ the female sits on the eggs.
- ◯ they run very fast.
- ◯ they are not Australian animals.

Grammar

Complete each sentence by adding an adjective to describe them.

green   busy   pretty   beautiful   yellow

a. The boy had a ______________ football jumper.

b. Emus lay ______________ eggs.

c. My mum has a ______________ face.

d. All the ladies were given a ______________ bunch of flowers.

e. The ______________ bees were buzzing around their hive.

Unit 17

Spelling

Look, cover, write, check each word.

word	write	check
stick	______________	☐
Australia	______________	☐
hatch	______________	☐
feather	______________	☐
female	______________	☐
gather	______________	☐
rather	______________	☐
caring	______________	☐

Word Building

Add **igh** to build word families.

igh

h___ ___ ___

n___ ___ ___t

s___ ___ ___t

l___ ___ ___t

fr___ ___ ___t

f___ ___ ___t

m___ ___ ___t

s___ ___ ___

t___ ___ ___t

he___ ___ ___t

kn___ ___ ___t

Spelling

Tick the word that is spelt correctly, then write it correctly on the line.

somtimes	sometims	sometimes	sumetimes	______________
inportant	important	importent	impurtent	______________
esplained	explaned	explained	esplaned	______________
afternoon	aftanoon	afttanoon	afternon	______________

3D Objects

Match each solid to its name.

a. 

b. 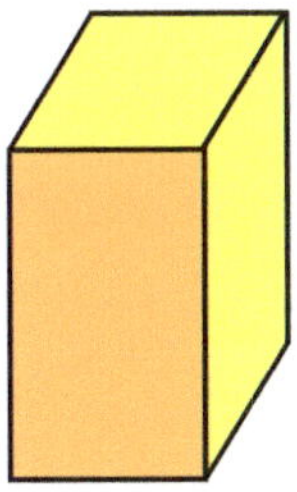

c. 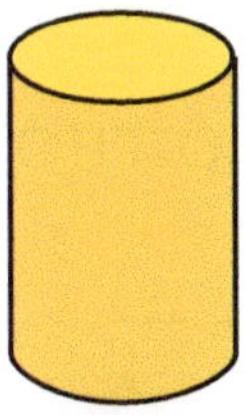

d. 

e. 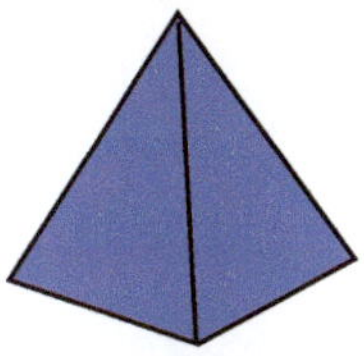

f. 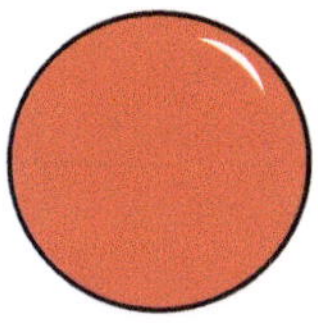

g. 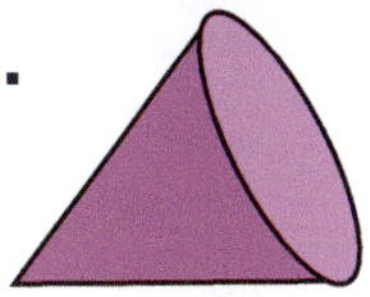

cylinder

cone

pyramid

rectangular prism

sphere

cube

hexagonal prism

Time

Draw a line from digital time to time in words.

a. 7 : 45	Quarter past eight
b. 3 : 15	Quarter to seven
c. 6 : 45	Quarter past three
d. 8 : 15	Quarter to three
e. 2 : 45	Quarter to eight

Wetlands

Have you ever seen a pond in a wetlands area? Often it seems quiet and peaceful, but it is a very busy place.

Small fish and animals dart from place to place in the water. Insects buzz about, moving between stems of plants. Frogs and turtles make a splash as they dive into the pond in search of food. At the bottom of the pond, other animals crawl and swim, looking for food, too.

Plants, insects, birds and animals live and feed around wetland ponds. Larger animals eat smaller ones, while others eat plants and insects. Every living thing in wetlands pond is food for some other animal, fish or bird.

Wetlands are important because they are the breeding grounds for wildlife, and they should be protected.

Understanding

Colour the bubble that best fits each sentence.

a. Wetlands are a busy place

- ◯ because people work there.
- ◯ because animals dart from place to place.
- ◯ there are lots of visitors.

b. Every living thing in wetlands

- ◯ needs a place to play.
- ◯ needs water.
- ◯ is food for some other animals.

Responding

a. Name three living things in a wetlands. ____________________

b. Name the wetlands near you. ____________________

c. What moves between stems of plants? ____________________

Spelling Rule

Some words that end in **o** need to add **es** to make them plural. Add **es** to make these words plural.

mosquito	tomato	dingo	volcano	potato
________	________	________	________	________

Sentence Ending

Add ending to these sentences.

Mosquitoes live ____________________

Mum cooked potatoes ____________________

I like tomatoes in ____________________

Spelling

Look, cover, write, check each word.

word	write	check
seen	______	☐
seem	______	☐
insect	______	☐
between	______	☐
plants	______	☐
large	______	☐
protect	______	☐
because	______	☐

Word Families

Add **ee** to build this word families.

ee

- f__ __l
- f__ __t
- b__ __
- tr__ __
- kn__ __
- thr__ __
- br__ __d
- qu__ __n
- st__ __l
- f__ __
- f__ __d
- s__ __n

Sentences

Unjumble these sentences.

a. I the visited wetlands. Today

____

b. wetlands. mosquitoes are There the of in lots

____

2D Shapes

Colour the shapes in each group that are **smaller** than the one in the box.

a.

b.

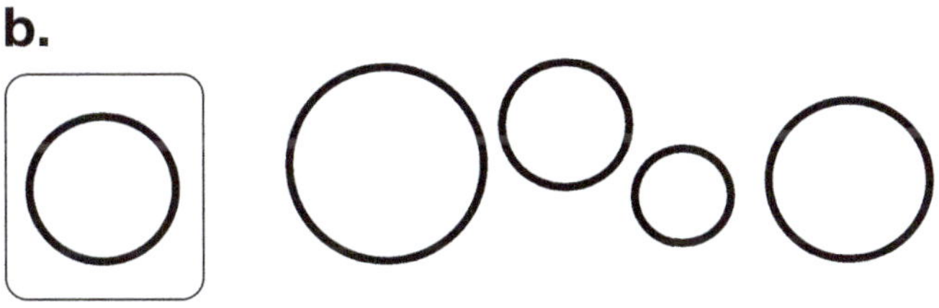

c.

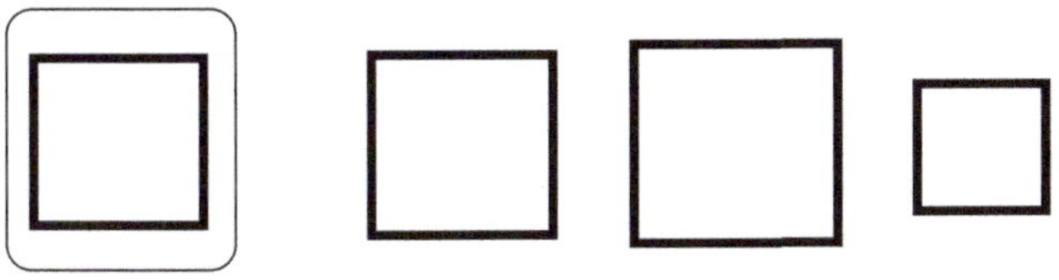

Multiplication

1. Write the number sentences for these.

a.

☐ x ☐ = ☐

b.

☐ x ☐ = ☐

2. Try these.

a. 3 x 5 = ☐

b. 2 x 7 = ☐

c. 10 x 3 = ☐

d. 5 x 6 = ☐

Rainforests

There are vast areas of rainforests in the world. Rainforests are usually found in warm areas where lots of rain falls during the year.

Trees and plants grow very fast in the warm forest. The floor of a rainforest is shady because the sun can't penetrate the canopy of trees. Vines hang joining tree tops to the forest floor. It is hot and sticky and the scent of a forest is like that of a damp cloth left in a sink on a hot day.

Trails of ants can be seen moving in all directions. Insects and small animals busy themselves gathering food. Lizards run up and down the trunks of trees while larger animals forage for food.

Chattering animals and the screech of birds that dwell in rainforests fill it with special forest sounds.

Understanding Colour the bubble that best fits the true statement.

a.
- ◯ Rainforests can be found everywhere.
- ◯ Rainforests occur where it is warm.
- ◯ Rainforests are open spaces.

b.
- ◯ Animals hang on vines.
- ◯ Plants grow very fast.
- ◯ Animals live in tree trunks.

Responding Use a dictionary to find the meaning of these words.

a. penetrate ______________________

b. canopy ______________________

c. scent ______________________

d. dwell ______________________

e. forage ______________________

f. Draw three animals that might live in a rainforest. Label them.

Unit 19

Spelling

Look, cover, write, check each word.

word	write	check
found	______	☐
during	______	☐
warm	______	☐
joining	______	☐
direction	______	☐
lizard	______	☐
birds	______	☐
sound	______	☐
noise	______	☐
paint	______	☐

Compound Words

Draw a line to join two words to make another word, then write the new word.

some	noon	______
cup	end	______
rain	ful	______
them	work	______
wet	one	______
week	self	______
after	forest	______
play	lands	______
your	selves	______
home	ground	______

Bar Chart Graph

Here is a bar chart showing items for sale in the local Aboriginal Gift Shop.

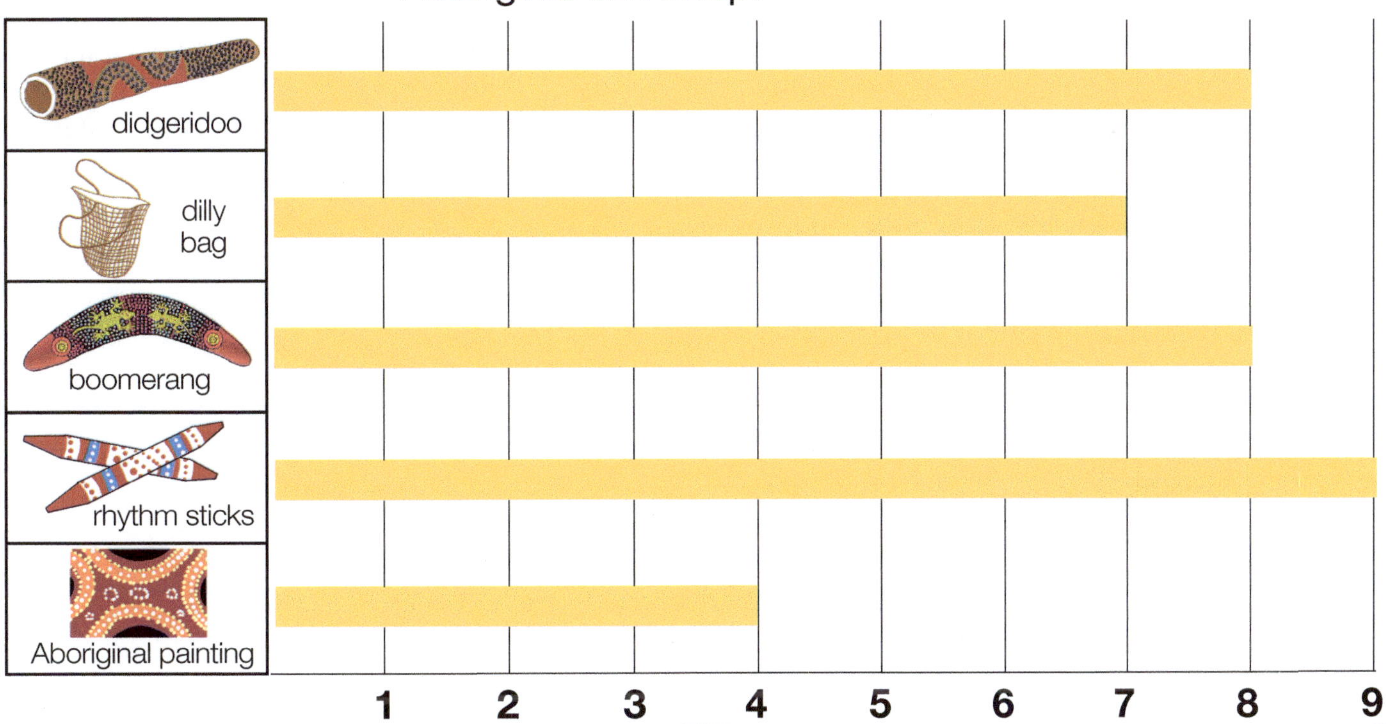

a. How many rhythm sticks for sale? ☐ **b.** How many paintings for sale? ☐

c. How many more didgeridoos than paintings for sale? ☐

d. Which items have the same amount for sale? ______

e. How many items in total for sale in the Gift Shop? ☐

A Shark at the Beach

Last Sunday my family went to the beach. Mum packed a picnic lunch, hats, towels and sunscreen. Dad put the chairs and umbrella from the garage in the boot.

When we set up, mum told us to stay close and only swim between the flags, so the life savers could see us.

All of a sudden an alarm started screeching.

"Out of the water!" yelled the lifesaver, "there is a shark just off the beach."

I saw the shark's fin coming towards me. My legs were going as fast as they could, but it's hard to run in water.

Suddenly, I felt something around my waist. I was in mid air. It was dad, he grabbed me and ran out of the water.

"You're safe now." he said "Come with us till the shark has gone."

I was shaking as I tried to eat my lunch.

Understanding Colour the bubble that best fits these sentences.

a. Mum was busy

- ◯ packing lunches and gear.
- ◯ sitting on the beach.
- ◯ swimming with the shark.

b. Swimming between the flags

- ◯ keeps sharks away.
- ◯ allows lifesavers to see you.
- ◯ a good place to have a lunch.

Interpreting Complete each sentence.

a. Dad packed the ________________________________

b. The lifesaver yelled ________________________________

c. Dad grabbed me and ________________________________

Grammar Pronouns take the place of nouns. Add these pronouns to a sentence.

Pronouns
She
He
We
They

a. Tom is Eight. ______ is having a birthday party.

b. I saw Mia and Paris. ________ were reading.

c. My sister is crying. ______ is sad.

d. ______ went to the football game.

Unit 20 Spelling

Look, cover, write, check each word.

word	write	check
family		☐
picnic		☐
towel		☐
close		☐
alarm		☐
beach		☐
shark		☐
lunch		☐
shake		☐

Double Letter Words

Add double **tt** or **pp** or **ll** or **dd** to focus on these words.

tt **pp** **ll** **dd**

ha__ __y

li __ __le

pu__ __y

ba __ __

ro __ __

ra __ __le

mi__ __le

wa __ __

co__ __on

ri __ __ le

pa__ __le

fi __ __ le

la __ __er

Health and P.E.

Circle the items most suitable to eat at breakfast time.

a.

b.

c.

d.

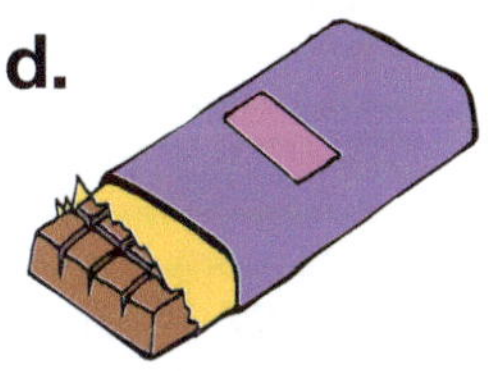

e.

f.

g.

h.

i.

j.

k.

l.

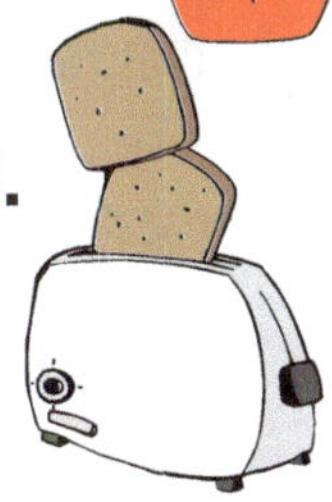

Addition

1. Fill in the missing numbers in each addition square.

a.

+			
	7		15
	12	9	
		17	36

b.

+			
	9		23
	15	7	
		21	45

2. Add number on the top to side numbers.

+	7	3	5	1	4	2	8
7							
5							

Time

Show the time on each clock face.

a.

quarter past nine

b.

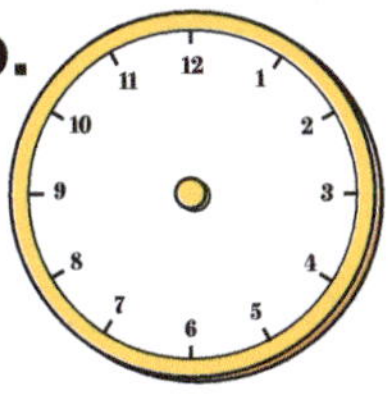

quarter past seven

c.

quarter past ten

d.

quarter to six

e.

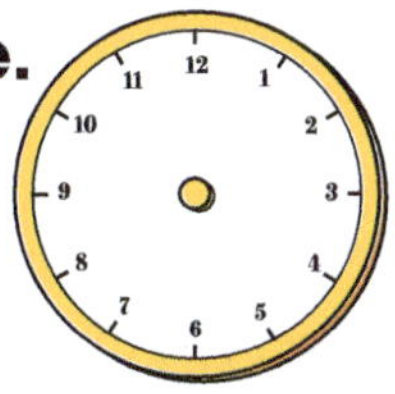

quarter to eleven

f.

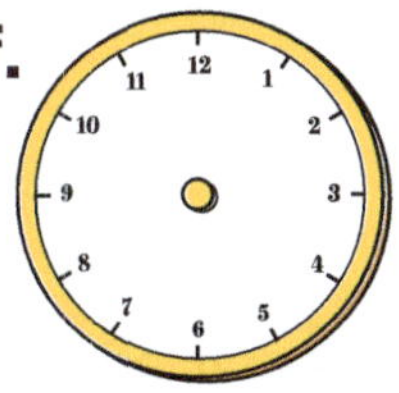

quarter to one

My home is Australia's great outback,
A long way off the beaten track.
I don't go to town too much, my friends are few,
But I'm busy and happy with lots to do.

I don't go to school - Mum teaches me.
We do reading and writing and three times three.
I listen each day to the School of the Air -
It's just like having my class-mates there.

At muster time I stay at Dad's side,
I've my own little motorbike to ride.
It's hot and dusty, but it's fun,
And I feel proud when the job's all done.

1. Write a title for this poem.

____

2. Write words from the poem that rhyme with:

a. track ________ ________

b. tree ________ ________

c. true ________ ________

d. none ________ ________

Match words from the poem to the correct meaning.

a. outback	an untarred, dusty road
b. track	having a good opinion of oneself
c. busy	always working
d. muster	away from other places
e. proud	gather animals together

Punctuation

Remember capital letters are used for Proper Nouns and sentence Beginnings. Add capital letters and full stops to correct the punctuation.

a. erin and paris went to sydney, last saturday, by train

____

b. we were in melbourne when the floods hit queensland

____

c. when dad was sick, he went to see doctor fred simkins

____

d. dr simkins sent him to hospital in brisbane for x-rays

____

Unit 21

Spelling

Look, cover, write, check each word.

word	write	check
town	____________	☐
great	____________	☐
busy	____________	☐
reading	____________	☐
proud	____________	☐
listen	____________	☐
poem	____________	☐
correct	____________	☐

Word Families

Add the **o-e** combination to write these words.

o-e

h__ p__
r __ p__
c __ n__
r __ b__
h __ s __
v __ t __
c __ d __
st__ n__
ph__ n__
r __ d __
n__ t __
wr__ t __

Sentences

Join these sentences using either **and**, **but** or **so**.

a. William was sick. He went to hospital.

____

b. It was early this morning. It is now afternoon.

____

c. Squeeze the orange juice. Pour it into the jug.

____

Ordinal Number

1. Write the order for each item.

2. Write the next ordinal numbers.

a. 29th ____________ **b.** 63rd ____________

c. 31st ____________ **d.** 40th ____________

e. 99th ____________ **f.** 22nd ____________

Place Value

1. What number is shown on each card?

a. ____________

b. ____________

c. ____________

2. Write the number shown on each abacus.

a.

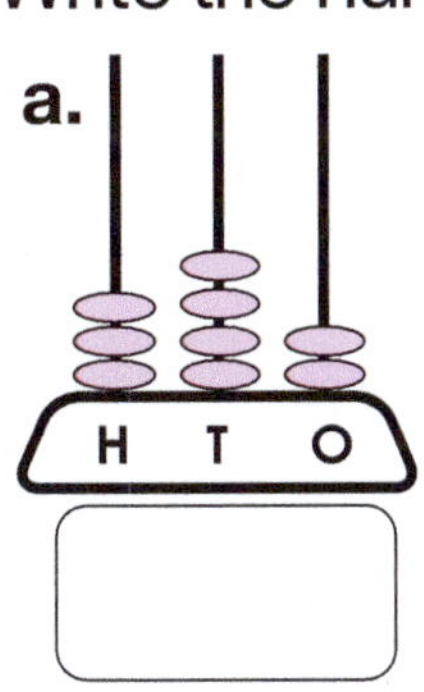

b.

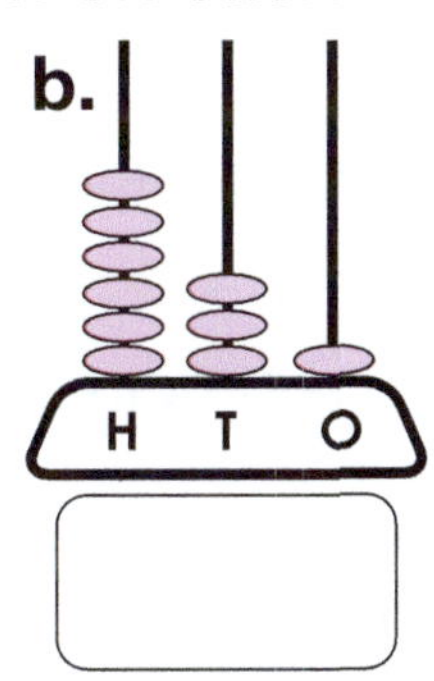

A Book Report

Kirt wrote a report about a book he enjoyed reading.

Do you read much?' I just finished reading a book about Australian Native Animals. There are hundreds of facts about our amazing native animals.

I liked to find information about the kangaroo. Did you know there are five kangaroos on our one dollar coin? Kangaroos can be found in every state and territory of Australia.

There are lots of photos of other animals throughout the book. There is a section where little flaps make each animal stand up. It also had easy to find information with pictures.

The book is really good because all the information is indexed alphabetically for easy use.

If you like finding out about Australian Native Animals you will like this book too! It is amazing!

Understanding Complete each sentence about Kirt's report.

a. The book was written by ____________________

b. Photographs were taken by ____________________

c. There are ____________________ on a one dollar coin.

d. In the section with little flaps ____________________

e. All the information is ____________________

f. Kirt thinks this book is ____________________

Interpreting Colour the box that best complete each sentence.

a. Kirt read the book [a long time ago] [a little while ago]

b. Australian Native Animals is [full of facts] [a made up story]

c. There are photographs [on some pages] [throughout the book]

d. Information in the book [is indexed alphabetically] [with pictures]

Unit 22

Spelling

Look, cover, write, check each word.

word	write	check
report	______________	☐
finish	______________	☐
hundred	______________	☐
amazing	______________	☐
facts	______________	☐
photograph	______________	☐
Australia	______________	☐
pictures	______________	☐

Word Families

Add the **oa** to build this word family.

oa

m __ __ n
c __ __ t
cr __ __ k
b __ __ t
s __ __ k
r __ __ d
cr __ __ k
cl __ __ k
m __ __ t
fl __ __ t
g __ __ t

Abbreviations

Sometimes words can be written in a shortened form. Road as Rd. Write these as abbreviations.

Street ______ Doctor ______ television ______ Mister ______

Misses ______ November ______ Avenue ______ Mistress ______

Kilometre ______ Centimetre ______ Reverend ______

Symmetry

Draw a line of symmetry on each shape or letter.

a.

b.
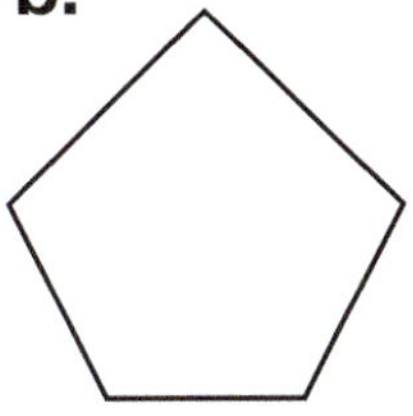
c.
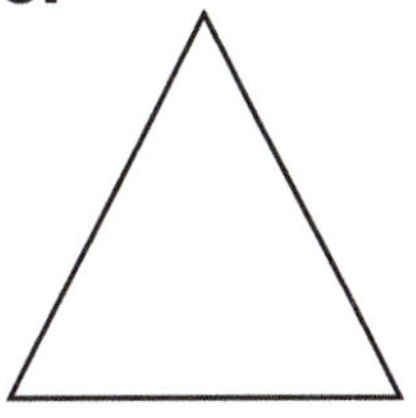
d.

e.
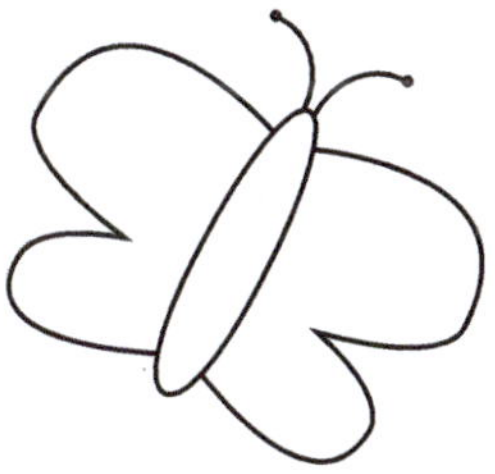
f.
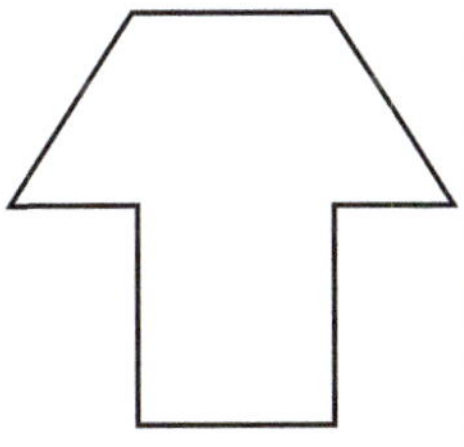
g.

Position

Here is a line of shapes. Write the position first to last of each shape.

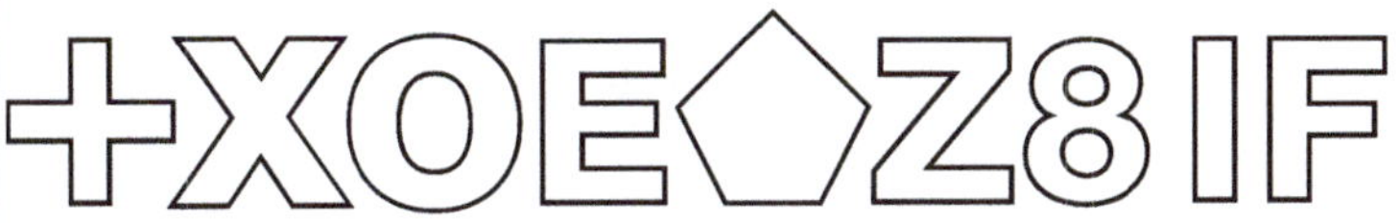

a. + ______ **b.** E ______ **c.** 8 ______

d. 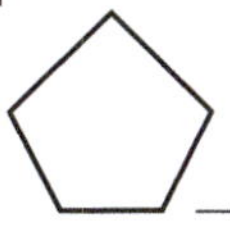 ______ **e.** O ______ **f.** X ______

g. Z ______ **h.** F ______ **i.** I ______

Aboriginal Legend

There are many myths and legends we hear from time to time. Here is a legend that helps explain how man found the boomerang.

Long ago, when the world was new, the sky-spirit sent rain upon the earth. The grass, plants and trees grew green and tall. But once, the sky-spirit sent too much rain and there was a great flood.

The earth-spirit threw a message stick into the sky to ask the sky-spirit to stop the rain. The sky-spirit threw it back! Again and again the earth-spirit threw it, but each time it came back.

The stick grew tired and rested on a rock. A young man picked it up. He threw it and it returned to him. The wise men said it was a gift from the sky-spirit to make up for the floods. That's how the boomerang came to us.

Understanding

Colour the bubble that best fits each question.

a. What did the sky-spirit send?

- ◯ rain
- ◯ snow
- ◯ the sun

b. Why did the message stick stop?

- ◯ the sky-spirit won
- ◯ the stick grew tired
- ◯ the young boy found it

Interpretation

Complete each sentence.

a. The sky-spirit sent ________________ for things to grow.

b. The message stick landed ______________________________.

c. The boomerang was a gift from ___________________________.

Punctuation

The exclamation mark (!) is used to show surprise, feeling or command. Add exclamation marks to the end of each one here.

a. Look out ____ **b.** Stop that ____ **c.** Take care ____

d. Ouch ____ **e.** Well done Ty ____ **f.** I said no ____

g. Don't do that ____ **h.** Jump off there ____ **i.** Oh dear ____

Spelling

Look, cover, write, check each word.

word	write	check
found	______	☐
world	______	☐
earth	______	☐
plants	______	☐
message	______	☐
threw	______	☐
young	______	☐
tired	______	☐

Word Building

Add **day** to build the time family.

to_ _ _ yester_ _ _

birth_ _ _ Sun_ _ _

Mon_ _ _ Tues_ _ _

Wed_ _ _ Thurs_ _ _

Fri_ _ _ Satur_ _ _

Mother's_ _ _ Father's_ _ _

Sentences

Unjumble these sentences.

a. need grass Trees to rain grow. and

____

b. many and There legends. myths are Aboriginal

____

c. is time you Do now? it know what

____

Counting Money

Find the value of each set by skip counting.

a. 

= $ ☐

b. 

= $ ☐

c. 

= $ ☐

Chance

Which is most likey to be picked from each bag?

a. 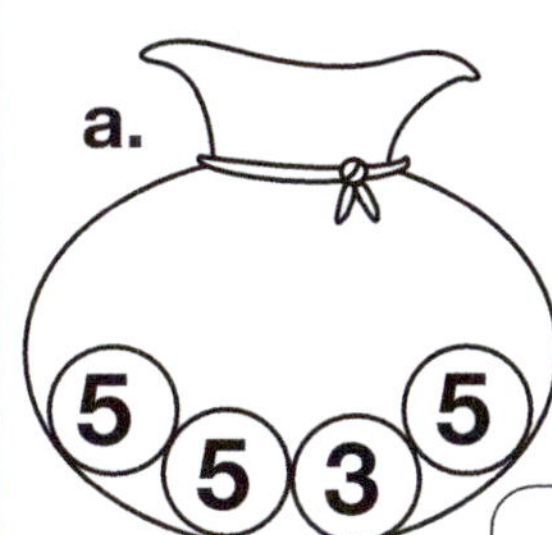

☐

b. 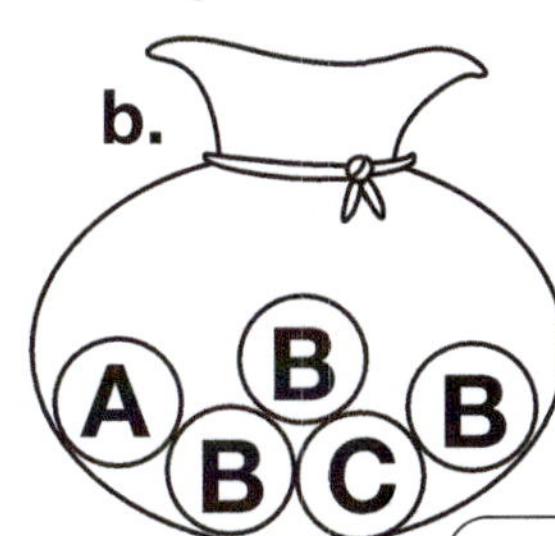

☐

c. 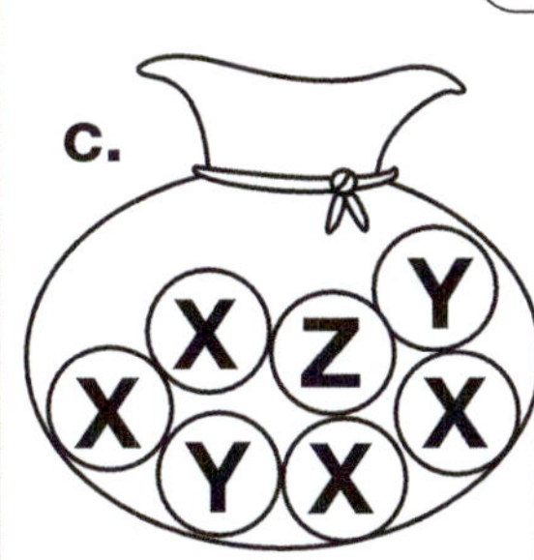

☐

d. 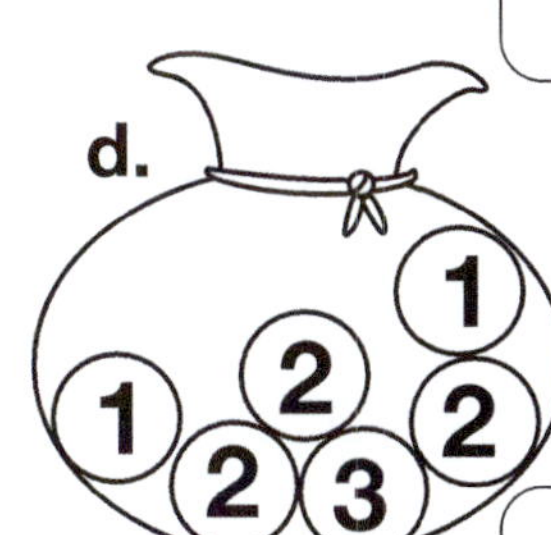

☐

Menu

Breads:	Garlic bread with herbs	$6
	Turkish bread with dips	$8
	Mini pizza bread with toppings	$4
Entrees:	Chicken nuggets with sauce	$6
	Soup and crispy bread roll	$5
Mains:	Hamburger with fries and sauce	$7
	Hot dog	$6
	Chicken burger with chunky chips	$7
	Pie with sauce and vegetables	$8
Desserts:	Jelly, fruit and ice cream	$4
	Chocolate sundae	$4
	Three flavours of ice cream with sprinkles	$4

Responding

Write a response for each question.

a. How much would it cost to have a mini pizza bread, chicken nuggets, a hotdog and chocolate sundae? ______________

b. What would you select if you had this menu?

____

c. How much would your meal cost? ______________

d. What meals don't you like to eat? ______________

____

Grammar

Adverbs tell **how, when, where** or why about a verb. They often end in "**ly**". Use the adverbs correctly in these sentences.

a. They run ______________ to the bus stop.

b. He walked ______________ to his room.

c. It was ______________ when the rain started.

d. The water dripped ______________ from tap.

Adverbs
upstairs
quickly
slowly
yesterday

Unit 24

Spelling

Look, cover, write, check each word.

word	write	check
pizza	____________	☐
chicken	____________	☐
soup	____________	☐
sauce	____________	☐
with	____________	☐
fruit	____________	☐
flavour	____________	☐
chocolate	____________	☐

Word Building

Add **ent** to build this word family.

ent

c__ __ __

b__ __ __

s__ __ __

d__ __ __

l__ __ __

sp__ __ __

w__ __ __

r__ __ __

t__ __ __

differ__ __ __

cem__ __ __

Sentences

Use words from the spelling list or word building to complete each sentence.

a. I like to eat ____________ when we go to the show.

b. Your pen is ____________ to mine.

c. Mum ____________ $7 when she bought the week's ____________ .

d. When I eat a pie, I like to add tomato ____________.

Hexagons

Colour the hexagons only.

a.

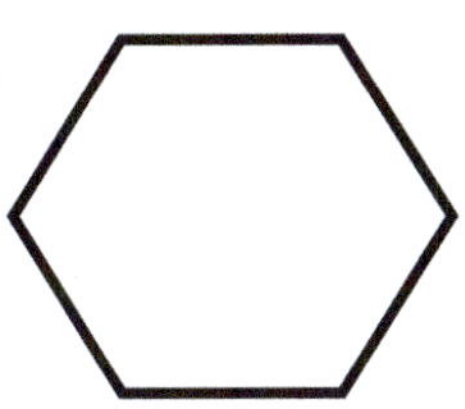

b.

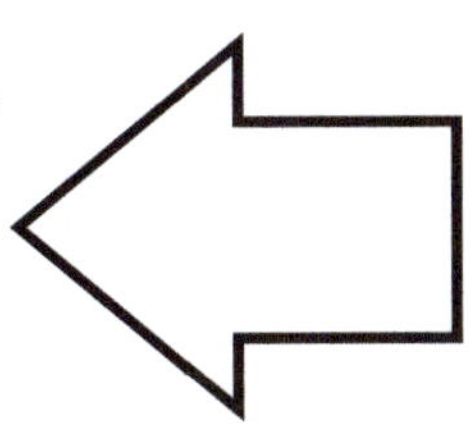

c.

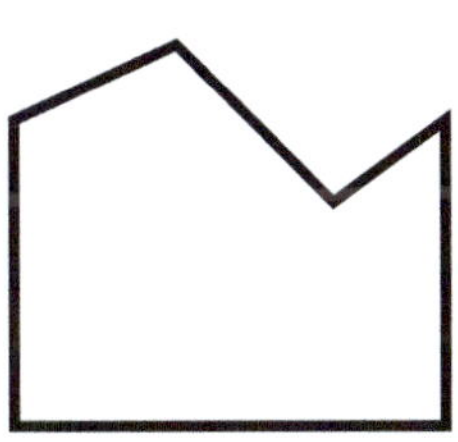

d.

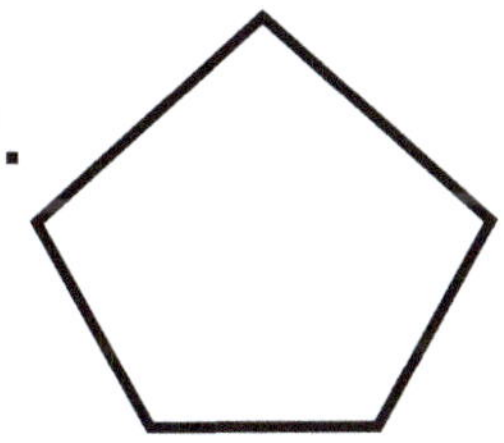

e.

Subtraction

1. Regroup ones to tens then find the difference.

a.

	T	O
	3	5
-	1	7

b.

	T	O
	6	4
-	2	8

c.

	T	O
	3	2
-	1	4

2. Subtract outside numbers from the web centre number.

start here

Going to School

The alarm was ringing. Six o'clock. Time to get up, make my bed, take a shower, get dressed, then have breakfast. After breakfast I pack my bag ready for school.

My sister and I leave home at seven o'clock in the ute. Mum takes us on the long trip to the bus stop. The bus picks us up and takes us to school.

The bus trip takes another hour to reach the school. We have lots of friends on the bus. They live on farms like we do. On the bus there is lots of chattering and singing. This helps the time pass quickly.

If I have a bad day at school the trip seems longer on the way home. Mum is usually waiting for us at the bus stop.

Understanding

Colour the bubble that best fits each sentence.

a. The trip from home to school takes

- ◯ one hour
- ◯ one and a half hours
- ◯ half an hour

b. What time does the bus pick up the children?

- ◯ seven o'clock
- ◯ eight o'clock
- ◯ half past seven

Word Puzzle

1. Find these types of transport in the word search.

C	A	R	B	D	H	F	I	M
P	M	Q	H	S	E	G	E	O
B	O	A	T	P	L	A	N	E
U	T	T	R	A	I	N	B	D
S	O	T	R	U	C	K	I	P
E	R	A	J	F	O	I	C	H
T	B	K	V	B	P	C	Y	Q
S	I	M	A	L	T	N	C	V
U	K	R	N	S	E	U	L	Z
V	E	T	W	X	R	Y	E	A

VAN
BUS
CAR
HELICOPTER
PLANE
BICYCLE
BOAT
MOTORBIKE
TRAIN
TRUCK

2. What am I?

a. I have 6 large wheels, with many places to sit. My driver collects fares.

I am a ____________________

b. I am big or small. I have wings and a tail. I take off.

I am a ____________________

c. I have a bow and a stern I can float.

I am a ____________________

Unit 25

Spelling

Look, cover, write, check each word.

word	write	check
alarm		
shower		
half		
reach		
another		
chatter		
waiting		
quickly		

Proof Reading

Proof read these sentences. Circle the misspelt word, then write it correctly.

a. Our car haz new tyres. ________

b. I came to shool by bus. ________

c. Mia road her bike today. ________

d. When I gro up I want to be a police officer. ________

e. Take care wen swimming. ________

f. Grandpa woz sixty last weekend. ________

g. Next weak I will be seven. ________

Sentences

Use some of the **ay** words to fill in the gaps of each sentence.

a. Every ________ I travel to school by bus.

b. I made a vase using ________ .

c. Dad drove down a one- ________ street.

d. I will ________ with my grandma tonight.

clay
stay
day
way

Regrouping

1. How many **tens** in each group?

a.

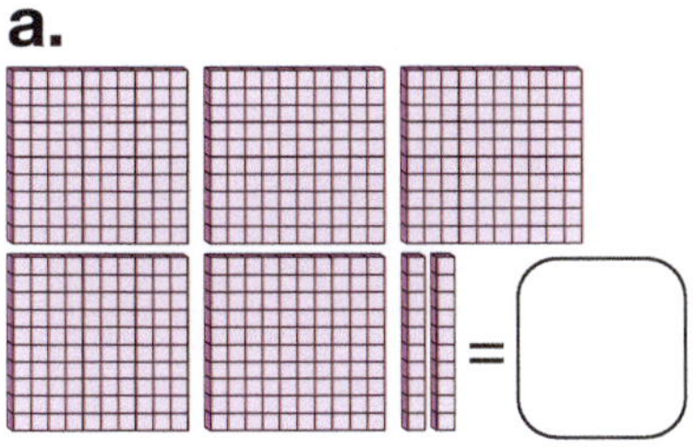

b.

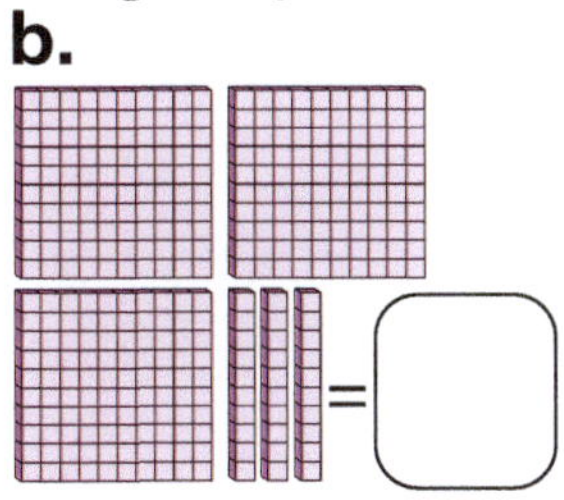

c.

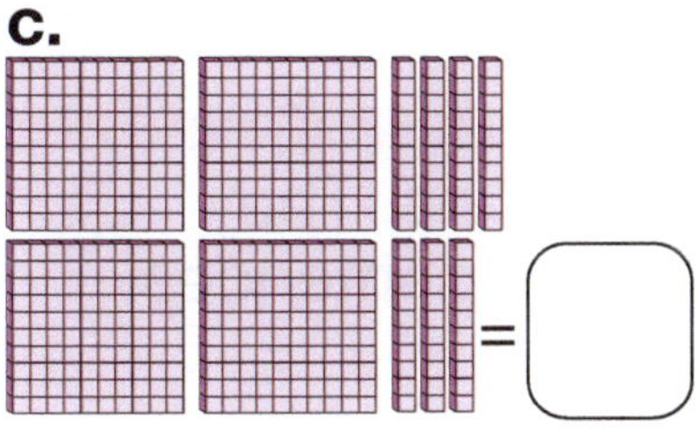

d.

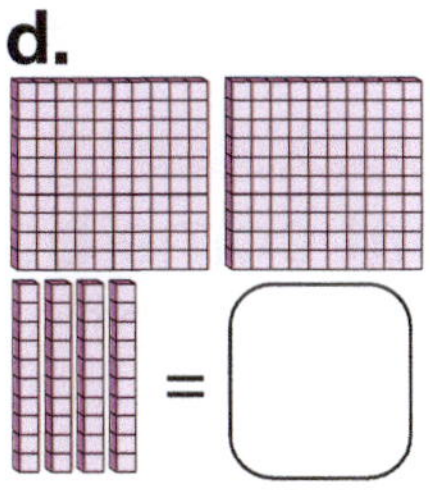

2. How many **ones** in each group?

a.

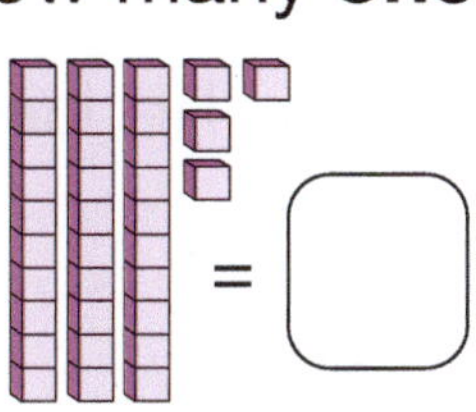

b.

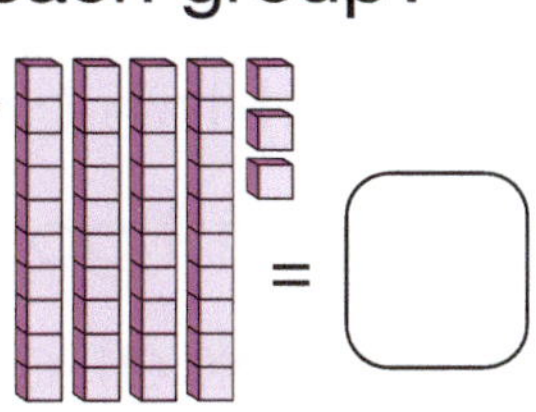

Chance

On which colour is the spinner likely to land?

a.

b.

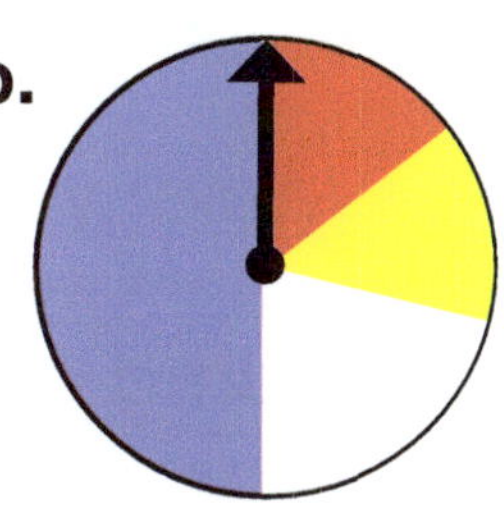

c.

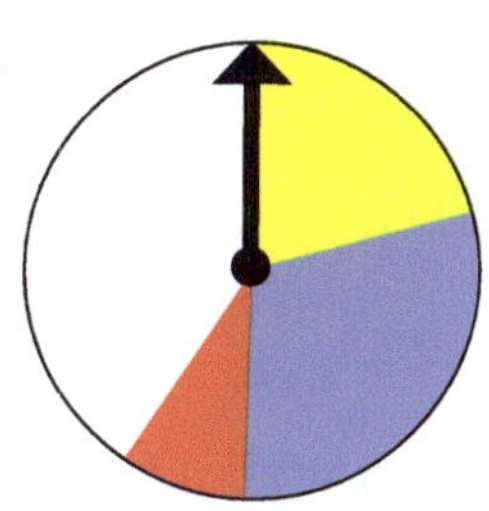

d.

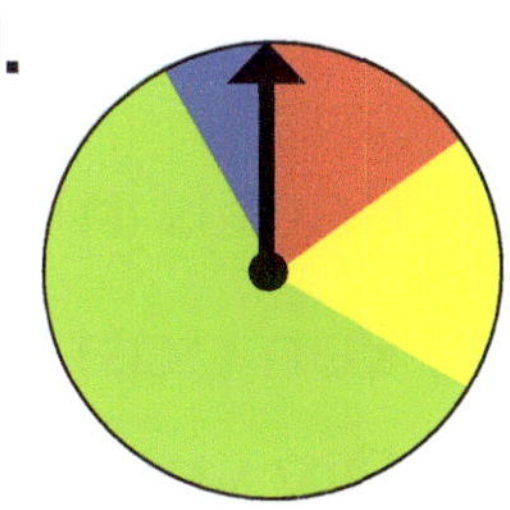

Mrs Malony

Mrs Maloney lives next door to my Grandma in Brisbane. She loves to work in her garden every day. Even when it rains Mrs Malony can be seen in her garden.

She has two fruit trees, one orange tree and a lemon tree. In the vegetable beds she grows vegetables and flowers.

Last Friday when I was at grandma's, Mr Malony brought in a basket of vegetables for grandma. There were beans, tomatoes, a lettuce and three cucumbers.

The two ladies sat down because grandma had made a cup of tea and a batch of scones. They chattered in between sipping tea and eating the scones. Grandma gave me a glass of milk and put cream and jam on my scone.

Grandma said Mrs Malony came in everyday for tea and a chat. She is good company for me when you're not here.

Understanding

Colour the bubble that best fits each sentence.

a. Who lives next door to Mrs Malony?

- ◯ the author
- ◯ grandma
- ◯ Mr Malony

b. What does grandma do for Mrs Malony?

- ◯ cooks her vegetables
- ◯ gives her a glass of milk
- ◯ makes tea and scones

Responding

Complete these sentences.

a. Mrs Malony is ______________________________

b. Grandma and Mrs Malony like to ______________________________

Grammar

Prepositions are small words that come before nouns. They tell where or when. Circle the prepositions in these sentences. One is done.

Paris is (in) the room.

a. Run past Simon.

b. Put the book under the bed.

c. Dry yourself in the bathroom.

d. Don't go near the fire.

e. William was on the boat.

f. Look after your sister.

Spelling

Look, cover, write, check each word.

word	write	check
next	______	☐
garden	______	☐
fruit	______	☐
vegetables	______	☐
basket	______	☐
tomato	______	☐
between	______	☐
company	______	☐

Word Building

Add **ay** to build this word family.

ay

d__ __
p __ __
st__ __
tod __ __
aw__ __
r__ __
sw__ __
tr __ __
cl__ __
pl __ __
l __ __
b__ __

Science and Technology

Computers are used every day. Tick those who might use computers.

butcher ☐	baker ☐	plumber ☐	builder ☐
doctor ☐	dentist ☐	teacher ☐	accountant ☐
miner ☐	student ☐	electrician ☐	police ☐

Multiplication

1. Write the number sentence for these.

☐ x ☐ = ☐

2. Complete these number sentences.

a. 3 × 5 = ☐ **b.** 5 × 6 = ☐

c. 2 × 7 = ☐ **d.** 3 × 8 = ☐

e. 5 × 8 = ☐ **f.** 10 × 4 = ☐

g. 2 × 9 = ☐ **h.** 5 × 9 = ☐

Division

1. Divide these bananas by 3.

☐ ÷ 3 = ☐

2. Complete these divisions.

a. 12 ÷ 2 = ☐ **b.** 20 ÷ 5 = ☐

c. 24 ÷ 3 = ☐ **d.** 30 ÷ 3 = ☐

e. 15 ÷ 5 = ☐ **f.** 16 ÷ 2 = ☐

g. 60 ÷ 10 = ☐ **h.** 27 ÷ 3 = ☐

My Sister

My big sister, Ashlee, likes to dance. She is a very good dancer. She has won lots of major prizes in competitions all over Australia. Her trophies are displayed all around her bedroom and in the lounge room.

Last week she won the biggest trophy I had ever seen and a trip to Canberra to dance in the National Finals. The National Finals are held in Canberra every year. Last year she came third in her age group. This year she is in the Open Titles. Mum says she has improved so much she could win the National Titles and a trip to England to dance in front of the Queen.

We are all excited about going to Canberra and possibly London.

Understanding Colour the bubble that does not fit each response.

a. Ashlee is
- ◯ a good dancer.
- ◯ older than the author.
- ◯ lives in Canberra.

b. The National Finals are held
- ◯ in London
- ◯ in front of the Queen
- ◯ in Canberra

Responding Complete each sentence.

a. Trophies are given ______________________________

b. Ashlee is going to Canberra ______________________________

Punctuation Add capital letters, full stops or question marks to these sentences.

a. my mum likes to visit canberra and melbourne

____

b. if you won a trip to england, would you take your sister

____

c. last week, william and kate visited grandma in Sydney

____

Unit 27

Spelling

Look, cover, write, check each word.

word	write	check
dance	____________	☐
prize	____________	☐
Australia	____________	☐
Canberra	____________	☐
England	____________	☐
London	____________	☐
Capital	____________	☐
excited	____________	☐

Compound Words

Draw a line to join two words to make a new word, then write the new word.

sun	times	____________
some	side	____________
help	fly	____________
butter	wave	____________
grass	day	____________
out	less	____________
micro	chair	____________
wood	hopper	____________
hand	ful	____________
high	lands	____________

Sentences

Unjumble these sentences.

a. Ashlee Sydney. Last to went week

____

b. older is cousin old. Tom My years ten

____

c. bought Mum new her Jo's skirt Dresses. at

____

Mass

Colour the one of each pair that is **heavier**.

a. 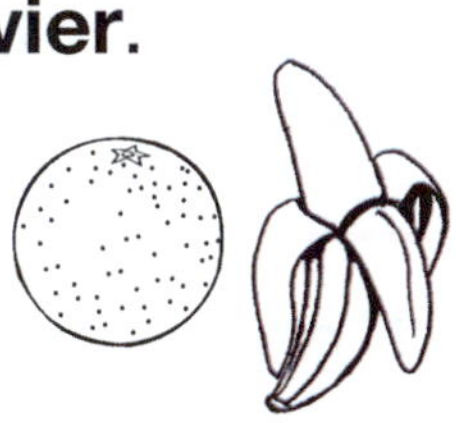

b. 

c. 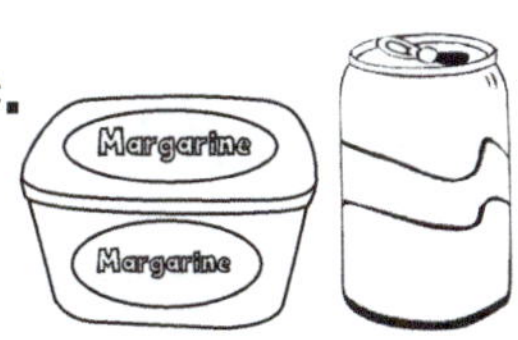

d. 

e. 

Time

Match each event to the best time.

a. 

b. 

c. 

d. 

Map Reading

Maps help us to travel. Look at the map, then complete the activities.

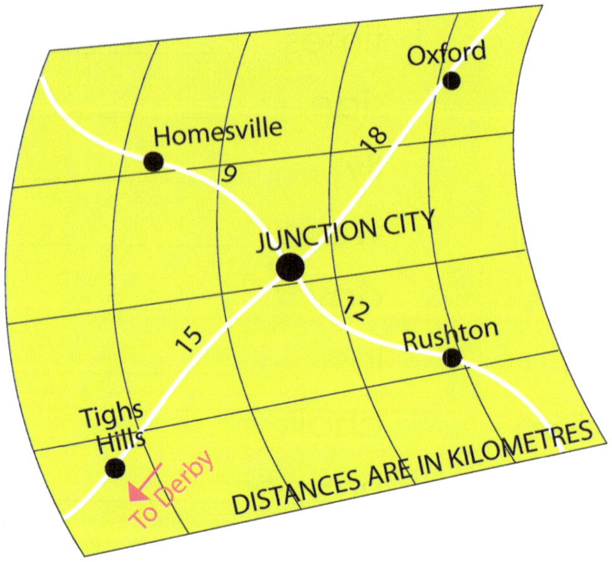

1. How many kilometres between Rushton and Junction City? ☐ km

2. What town would I pass through if I went from Junction City to Derby?

   ____

3. How far is it from Homesville to Oxford by road? ☐ km

Spelling

Look, cover, write check each word.

word	write	check
travel	____________	☐
distance	____________	☐
holiday	____________	☐
would	____________	☐
could	____________	☐
should	____________	☐

Word Meanings

Find the meaning of each word.

a. trek ______________________________

____

b. explore ______________________________

____

c. extinct ______________________________

____

d. character ______________________________

____

Sentences

Time connections begin sentences and tell us **when, then, now, after**. Add a **time connection** to the following sentences.

a. ______________ we travelled to Tighs Hill.

b. ______________ we had stayed in Junction City.

c. ______________ my brother is in hospital.

d. ______________ it is my turn with the iPad.

e. ______________ mum is picking the car.

Connectives

- Meanwhile
- At this time
- Before that
- Last week
- Now

Reading

Timetable

Here is a bus timetable. Look at it closely, then complete the activities.

STOPS	TIMES						
JUNCTION	8:00	8:30	9:00	9:30	10:00	10:30	11:00
SCHOOL	8:15	8:45	9:15	9:45	10:15	10:45	11:15
POOL	8:20	8:50	9:20	9:50	10:20	10:50	11:20
SUPER MARKET	8:30	9:00	9:30	10:00	10:30	11:00	11:30
TOWN HALL	8:45	9:15	9:45	10:15	10:45	11:15	11:45
CIVIC	8:50	9:20	9:50	10:20	10:50	11:20	11:50
CINEMA	9:00	9:30	10:00	10:30	11:00	11:30	12:00
RAILWAY STATION	9:10	9:40	10:10	10:40	11:10	11:40	12:10

1. How often do the buses leave Junction? ______________________

2. How long does it take to go from Junction to the Cinema? ______________________

3. What time bus must I catch to get from Junction to Railway Station by 12:10? ______________________

4. How many stops does a bus have on its route? ☐

Chance

Draw a line from each picture to the chance it could happen.

a.

b.

c.

d.

certain

likely

impossible

possible

unlikely

Spelling

Look, cover, write check each word.

word	write	check
likely	______________	☐
certain	______________	☐
favourite	______________	☐
cousin	______________	☐
trouble	______________	☐
caught	______________	☐

Grammar

Articles: Indefinite articles are a and an. The definite article is **the**. Circle the articles in these sentences, then write it and the noun it identifies.

a. Ashlee always has an egg for breakfast. ______________________

b. The shops close at half past ten. ______________________

c. I read a book last night. ______________________

d. We went to the cinema last Saturday. ______________________

e. Diana took an orange to school. ______________________

Time - Months

Here is a calendar for winter. It is not this year's calendar.

June

S	M	T	W	T	F	S	S	M	T	W	T	F	S
				1	2	3	4	5	6	7	8	9	10
11	12	13	14	15	16	17	18	19	20	21	22	23	24
25	26	27	28	29	30								

July

S	M	T	W	T	F	S	S	M	T	W	T	F	S
						1	2	3	4	5	6	7	8
9	10	11	12	13	14	15	16	17	18	19	20	21	22
23	24	25	26	27	28	29	30	31					

August

S	M	T	W	T	F	S	S	M	T	W	T	F	S
									1	2	3	4	5
6	7	8	9	10	11	12	13	14	15	16	17	18	19
20	21	22	23	24	25	26	27	28	29	30	31		

1. On what day of the week does winter finish? ______________

2. What day is 1st July? ______________

3. What are the dates for the first weekend in winter?

______________ ______________

4. What is the day and date for the last day of autumn?

______________ ______________

5. How many Saturdays in July? ☐

6. What are the dates for the last weekend in winter?

______________ ______________

7. How many days in winter? ☐

8. Do you like winter? Yes ☐ No ☐

9. What is the date for the first day of spring? ______________

Spelling

Look, cover, write check each word.

word	write	check
Autumn	______________	☐
weekend	______________	☐
finish	______________	☐
winter	______________	☐
starting	______________	☐
beautiful	______________	☐
please	______________	☐

Spelling

Use verbs to argue a position or point: **could, should, must, would.**

a. You __________ help with chores.

b. It __________ be good to help you.

c. You __________ think about that.

d. You __________ learn to save money.

e. It __________ stop the bus that way.

Punctuation

Add inverted commas to the speech in these sentences. (“ ”)

a. Did you wash that dish? asked mum.

b. Have you any money? he asked.

c. No! It wasn't me. he said.

d. Are you ready yet? asked dad.

e. Look out! he yelled.

f. Come here now! called mum.

Answers

<table>
<tr><td>Unit 1</td><td>Understanding: a. of different animals. b. gentle lambs and cute moneys. c. are like the real homes in the jungle or plain. / Interpreting: a. Yes, b. Yes, c. No, d. No / Grammar: a. elephant b. telephone c. giraffe d. kangaroo e. zebra f. lamb g. lion / Spelling: Parent / Word Building: book, cook, rook, shook,wood, foot, stood, wool, look, hook, took / Sentences: a. Amy sat on the elephant's back. b. Paris nursed a baby lamb. c. We had lunch with the animals. d. Our class might visit the zoo. / Counting on: a. 9+8=17, b. 4+10=14, c. 6+12=18, / Numbers 1-100: 1a. 6,12 b.12, 18 / 2a. 48 b. 71, c. 69.</td></tr>
<tr><td>Unit 2</td><td>Understanding: a. caravan, b. gas stove, c. who catch the bus, d. on the bus about 4pm. / Interpreting: a. in a big annex b. the park manager gets upset (noise) c. near the office / Grammar: a. Close b. Open c. Spread d. Cut / Spelling: Parent / Word Building: tool, soon, room, broom, school, spoon, moon, pool, fool / Punctuation: Sunday, Monday, Tuesday, Wednesday, Thursday, Friday, Saturday / 3D Objects: a. cube, b. rectangular prism, c. cylinder, d. cylinder, e. cone, f. rectangular prism, g. shere, f. cone / Location:
<table>
<tr><td>□</td><td></td><td></td><td></td><td></td></tr>
<tr><td></td><td></td><td></td><td>○</td><td></td></tr>
<tr><td></td><td></td><td></td><td>△</td><td></td></tr>
<tr><td></td><td></td><td>⬡</td><td></td><td></td></tr>
<tr><td></td><td></td><td></td><td></td><td></td></tr>
</table></td></tr>
<tr><td>Unit 3</td><td>Understanding: a. to protect your head, b. borrow one, c. it is the law, d. common sense. / Interpreting: a. fits tightly b. safety rules c. wear a helmet / Grammar: a. blue sky b. green grass c. fluffy clouds d. big dog e. tall building f. fast car / Spelling: parent/ Word Building: saw, raw, jaw, straw, claw, thaw, law, draw, paw/ Road Safety: a. stop b. Give way c. Keep left d. Walk carefully / Time: 1a. 5:00 b. 3:30 c. 9:30 2. a. 7:30 b. 8:00 c. 6:00 d. 9:30 / Addition: 1a. 12 b. 15 c. 12 d.15 e.15 f. 17, 2a. 16, 10, 9, 14, 13, 18, 19 b. 13, 7, 6, 11, 10, 15, 16 c. 17, 11, 10, 15, 14, 19, 20.</td></tr>
<tr><td>Unit 4</td><td>Responding: a. by, sky, b. puddle, c. along, d. me, e. are, f. fun, one / Interpreting: snake, birds, kangaroos, platypus, wombat, kookaburra, emu / Sentences: a. How old are you? b. I like Australian animals. c. Koala's are my favourite. d. Do you like visiting the zoo? e. Do you get cold? f. Gum trees are very big. / Spelling: Parent / Word Building: crow, blow, window, flow, grow, mow, bow, show, know, slow / Opposites: day, low, dull, later, sad, long, front, no / Subtraction:1a. 8 b. 5 c. 8 d. 5 e. 6 f. 6 g. 8 h. 13 / 2. 14-6=8cards / Fractions: 1a. 4 b. 3 c. 5 d.4 /2.a. 3/4 b. 3/8 c. 2/6=1/3.</td></tr>
<tr><td>Unit 5</td><td>Understanding: a. jumps and chases sticks. b. hears the post lady's bike. c. sometimes d. every day / Interpreting: a. young b. he sees the post lady. / Punctuation: a. I, I, Rex, . b. Do Oscar ? / Spelling: Parent / Word Building: car, tar, card, start, dark, shark, smart, mark, bark, star, far, bar / Sentences: a. car, tar, dark, b. card, mark, c. star, dark / Mass: e., a., d., b., f., c., g. / Groups: a. 6, 6. 2 groups of 6=12, b. 6, 6, 6. 3 groups of 6=18</td></tr>
<tr><td>Unit 6</td><td>Understanding: a. Saturday. b. Pony rides. c. big d. magician / Interpreting: Adult: Hoopla, Lucky dips, Knock'em down, Book sale, Tea and Coffee, Uniform sale / Children: Jumping Castle, Toffee stall, Face Painting, Pony rides, Sausage sizzle, Super Hebert/ Both: Answers will vary - parent to check. / Spelling: Parent / Word Building: meat, read, sleat, cream, speak, steak, treat, beads, peach, seat / Sentences: a. My family are going to the Monster Fete on Saturday. b. Dad is cooking a sausage sizzle on the BBQ. c. I will go on a Pony Ride at the fete. / Money:1. a. ten cents b. two dollars c. one dollar 2. $2.75 / Lines: a. curved b. crossed lines c. parallel lines d. zig zag e. horizontal f. broken.</td></tr>
<tr><td>Unit 7</td><td>Understanding: a. my birthday. b. to buy party food. c. the fun games. d. I am turning eight. / Responding: a. Saturday b. school, soccer team c. food, fun games, party. / Writing: Parent / Spelling: Parent / Word Building: sing, cling, thing, ring, sting, ping, cling, bring, wing, king, ding, swing / People Who Help Us: a. paramedic b.doctor c. fireman d. teacher e. nurse f. police officer / Addition:1. a. 98 b. 57 c. 69 2. $23+$44=$67 / Area: a. 17 b. 20 c. 24.</td></tr>
<tr><td>Unit 8</td><td>Understanding: a. brother and sister. b. at the Theme Park. c. Mrs Holmes. d. a letter. / Interpreting: a. Belltown b.NSW 2222. / Punctuation: a. My/Ellie/ . b. My/Mrs Holmes/ . c. Do/Queensland/ ? / Spelling: Parent / Word Building: brother, letter, flower, father, fern, winter, tier, summer, paper, mother, sister / Opposites: out, slow, old, up, bad, first, last, big, back, tame, night, sad / Patterns:1. a. 6, 12, 14 b. 9, 18, 27 c. 25, 40, 45 2. a. 15, b. 12, c. 20, d. 18 e. 13 f. 26 / Time: a-C, b-A, c-D, d-B.</td></tr>
</table>

Answers

Unit 9	**Understanding: a.** At the Show Ground **b.** teenagers pushing each other **c.** get a discount **d.** four races. / **Interpreting: a.** friends **b.** the way home / **Grammar: a.** fast **b.** carefully **c.** quickly **d.** noisily / **Spelling:** Parent / **Word Building:** fork, horse, pork, force, explorer, stork, fort, corn, cord, cork / **Sentences: a.** with my friend William, **b.** tickets for four races. **c.** waiting to buy tickets. **d.** we ate a pie. / **Flip, Slide, Turn: a.** slid along **b.** turned around **c.** flipped over. / **Money: a.** $65 **b.** $80
Unit 10	**Reading: a.** angry **b.** no **c.** 30 **d.** 12 **Grammar: a.** Stop **b.** Ask **c.** Spread **d.** Get **e.** Cut / **Punctuation: a.** Today, Wednesday, Jon, Luna Park⊙ **b.** Paris, Alex, Perth⊙ / **Spelling:** Parent / **Word Building:** olled, rained, locked, cheered, laughed, yelled, barked, walked, handed, talked, washed / **Sentences: a.** Myths and legends tell old time stories. **b.** I like to visit my grandma in Melbourne. / **Mass: a.** down **b.** up / **Time:** a. b. c. d. e. f. 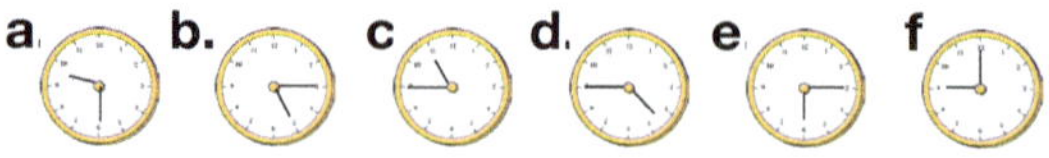
Unit 11	**Responding:** Answers will vary: **a.** grin **b.** away **c.** tall **d.** grass, class / **Meanings: a.** waste material **b.** use again **c.** the world around us **d.** very important **e.** keep things safe or the same **f.** a big smile / **Writing:** Parent / **Sentences: a.** Plant a tree and make Australia green. **b.** Recycle paper and help save a tree. / **Spelling:** Parent / **Word Building:** rain, pain, sail, snail, train, grain, gain, drain, brain, paint, nail / **Pollution: bx, cx, ex, fx, a ✓ d✓** / **Capacity: 1. b., d., f. 2.** bucket / **Subtraction: 1a.** 5 **b.** 4 **c.** 2 **d.** 9 **2.** 4, 3, 8, 5, 6
Unit 12	**Understanding: a.** ride his bike in the park **b.** the rain will stop soon **c.** hurry up **d.** get wet. / **Interpreting: a.** Simon **b.** Saturday **c.** The Park / **Punctuation: a.** "I think it is going to rain tomorrow". **b.** "Will you take me to the shops to buy new shoes?" **c.** "Tell me more about the new bike." **d.** "Hurray, hurray, I think we won lotto.!" / **Spelling:** Parent / **Word Building:** cake, rake, bake, wake, shake, flake, lake, snake, take, make / **Sentences:** Parent / **Place Value: 1a.** 783 **b.** 409 **c.** 567 **2.a.** 325, **b.** 402 **c.** 724 / **Addition: 1a.** 479 **b.** 758 **c.** 859 **d.** 848 **e.** 579 **f.** 498 **2.** $198
Unit 13	**Understanding: a.** To show how to say it **b.** Bacteria **c.** By washing our clothes **d.** Washing your face, hands, cleaning your teeth and wearing clean clothes. / **Interpreting:** Answers will vary. Parent / **Spelling:** Parent / **Word Building:** brick, clock, sock, click, stack, bucket, pocket, rocket, stuck, sick, sack, stick, duck / **Spelling: a.** pocket, **b.** remove, **c.** daily, d. yourself, sick / **Area: a.** 22 **b.** 24 / **More Money: a.** $38.50 **b.** $80.95 **c.** $34.85
Unit 14	**Response: a.** Southern hemisphere. **b.** Winter. **c.** Winter. / **Our Seasons:** Parent / **Opposites: a.** winter **b.** low **c.** top **d.** cold **e.** close/shut **f.** small **g.** south / **Plurals:** hats, dogs, chairs, years, months, cats, seasons, days, lizards, boys / **Spelling:** Parent / **Word Building:** bird, skirt, first, circus, birthday, shirt, squirt, thirty, thirsty, dirt, girl, third / **Groupings: a.** colours, **b.** months, **c.** seasons, **d.** children **e.** fruit **f.** games/sport /A **Subtraction: a.** 13 **b.** 28 **c.** 55 **d.** 16 **e.** 28 / **Fractions: a.** 1/4 **b.** 3/4 **c.** 1/2 **d.** 1/8
Unit 15	**Understanding: a.** it is cleaned **b.** polluted water / **Interpreting:** Answers will vary. Parent / **Abbreviations:** he'll, she's, hasn't, we're, isn't, don't, haven't, I'll, she'll / **Plurals:** busses, classes. dresses, foxes, churches, boxes, matches, wishes, dishes, fixes, **Spelling:** Parent. / **Word Building:** mouse, our, loud, cloud, sound, proud, round, hound, shout, about, out, house / **Sentences: a.** every day living. **b.** can become polluted. **c.** by drinking polluted water. **d**Hbefore it comes out of the tap. / **Length:** Answers will vary. / **Corners and Edges: 1a. b. c. d.** All four corners and four edges. **2.** Yes.
Unit 16	**Understanding: a.** By ambuance **b.** after four o'clock / **Responding:** Answers will vary. Parent / **Punctuation: a.** Dad, Erin, Kate⊙ b. The Dr Fuller⊙ c. Was, Erin, Kates ? d. Kate, Barton High School, Canberra⊙ / **Spelling:** Parent. / **Word Building:** date, gate, rate, state, slate, create, plate, mate, late, / **Our Community:**  **Number: a.** 12 **b.** 60 **c.** 18 **d.** 70 / **2D Shapes: a.**  **b.**  **c.**  **d.** 

Answers

Unit 17	**Understanding: b.** ✓ **c.** ✓ **e.** ✓ **f.** ✓ **h.** ✓ **/ Interpreting: a.** last weekend **b.** the female sits on the eggs **/ Grammar: a.** yellow **b.** green **c.** pretty **d.** beautiful **e.** busy **/ Spelling:** Parent **/ Word Building:** night, light, fight, sigh, height, knight, tight, might, fright, sight, high **/ Spelling:** sometimes, important, explained, afternoon. / **3D Objects: a.** cube **b.** rectangular prism **c.** cylinder **d.** hexagonal prism **e.** pyramid **f.** sphere **g.** cone **/ Time: a.** quarter to eight **b.** quarter past three **c.** quarter to seven **d.** quarter past eight **e.** quarter to three.
Unit 18	**Understanding: a.** because animals dart from place to place **b.** is food for other animals **/ Responding:** Answers will vary. Parents. **/ Spelling Rule:** mosquitoes, tomatoes, dingoes, volcanoes, potatoes. **/ Sentence Ending:** Answers will vary. Parents. **/ Spelling:** Parent **/ Word Families:** seen, feed, fee, steel, queen, breed, three, knee, tree, bee, feet, feel **/ Sentences: a.** Today I visited the wetlands. **b.** There are lots of mosquitoes in the wetlands. **/ 2D Shapes: a.** 1st **b.** 2nd and 3rd **c.** last **/ Multiplication: 1a.** 2x5=10 **b.** 3x4=12 **2a.** 15 **b.** 14 **c.** 30 **d.** 30.
Unit 19	**Understanding: a.** Rainforests occur where it's warm. **b.** Plants grow very fast. **/ Responding: a.** Penetrate - to go through. **b.** Canopy - overhead cover. **c.** Scent - smell. **d.** Dwell - live **e.** Forage - search for food. **f.** Parents. **/ Spelling:** Parent **/ Compound Words:** someone, cupful, rainforest, themselves, wetlands, weekend, afternoon, playground, yourself, homework **/ Bar Chart Graph: a.** 9 **b.** 4 **c.** 4 more **d.** didgeridoo and boomerang. **e.** 36
Unit 20	**Understanding: a.** packing lunches and gear. **b.**Állows life savers to see you. **/ Interpreting: a.** chairs and umbrella in the boat **b.** Out of the water! There's a shark just off the beach. **c.** ran out of the water **/ Grammar: a.** He **b.** They **c.** She **d.** He **/ Spelling:** Parent **/ Double Letter Words:** happy, little, puppy, ball, roll, rattle, middle, wall, cotton, riddle, paddle, fiddle, latter **/ Health and PE: a., b., c., e., i., k., l., / Addition: a.** 8, 21, 19 **b.** 14, 22, 14 / **2.a.** 14, 10, 12, 8, 11, 9, 15, **b.** 12, 8, 10, 6, 9, 7, 13. **Time: a.**  **b.**  **c.** 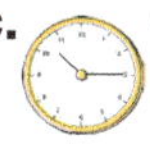 **d.**  **e.**  **f.** 
Unit 21	**Reading: 1.** Parent **2.a.** outback **b.** me tree **c.** few, do **d.** fun, done **/ Matching: a.** away from other places, **b.** untarred, dusty road. **c.** always working, **d.** gathering animals together, **e.** having a good opinion of oneself. **/ Punctuation: a. E**rin, **P**aris, **S**ydney, **S**aturday⊙ **b. W**e, **M**elbourne, **Q**ueensland⊙ **c. W**hen, **D**r **F**red **S**imkins⊙ **d. D**r Simkins, **B**risbane⊙ **/ Spelling:** Parent **/ Word Family:** hope, robe, vote, stone, rode, wrote, note, phone, code, hose, cone, rope **/ Sentences: a.** so **b.** but **c.** and **/ Ordinal Number: 1.** 2nd, 3rd, 5th, 6th **2.a.** 30th **b.** 64th **c.** 32nd **d.** 41st **e.** 100th **f.** 23rd **/ Place Value: 1.a.** 487 **b.** 296 **c.** 503 **2.a.** 342 **b.** 631
Unit 22	**Understanding: a.** Russell Smith. **b.** Scott Fisher. **c.** 5 kangaroos **d.** animals stand up. **e.** alphabetical. **f.** amazing. **/ Interpreting: a.** a little while ago. **b.** full of facts. **c.** throughout the book. **d.** is indexed alphabetically. **/ Spelling:** Parent **/ Word Families:** goat, float, moat, cloak, croak, road, soak, boat, croak, coat, moan **/ Abbreviations:** St, Dr, TV, Mr, Mrs, Nov, Ave, Miss, km, cm, Rev. **/ Symmetry: a.**  **b.**  **c.** 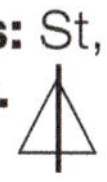 **d.** 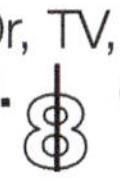 **e.**  **f.**  **g.** 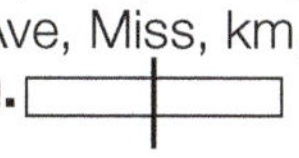 / Á **Position: a. 1**st **b.** 4th **c.** 7th **d.** 5th **e.** 3rd **f.** 2nd **g.** 6th **h.**9th **i.** 8th
Unit 23	**Understanding: a.** rain **b.** the stick grew tired **/ Interpretation: a.** rain **b.** on the rock. **c.** the sky-spirit. / **Punctuation:** All need ! for exclamation. **/ Spelling:** Parent **/ Word Building:** today, yesterday, birthday, Sunday, Monday, Tuesday, Wednesday, Thursday, Friday, Saturday, Mother's Day, Father's Day **/ Sentences: a.** Trees and grass need rain to grow. **b.** There are many Aboriginal myths and legends. **c.** Do you know what time it is now? **/ Counting Money: a.** \$20 **b.** \$100 **c.** \$300 **/ Chance: a.** 5 **b.** B **c.** x **d.** 2
Unit 24	**Reading: a.** \$20 b. Parent to check. **c.** Parent **d.** Parent **/ Grammar: a.** quickly **b.** upstairs. **c.** yesterday **d.** slowly **/ Spelling:** Parent **/ Word Building:** bent, dent, spent, rent, different, cement, tent, went, lent, sent, cent, **/ Sentences: a.** pizza/fruit/chocolate. **b.** different. **c.** spent, fruit **d.** sauce **/ Hexagons: a., c., e. Subtractions: 1.a.** 18 **b.** 36 **c.** 18 **2.** 51, 43, 56, 54, 52, 40, 37, 59, 48.

Answers

Unit 25	**Understanding: a.** one and a half hours **b.** half past seven **/ Word puzzle:** Parent - enjoy. **2.a.** bus **b.** plane **b.** ship or boat **/ Spelling:** Parent. **/ Proof Reading: a.** has **b.** school **c.** rode **d.** grow **e.** when **f.** was **g.** week **Sentences: a.** day **b.** clay **c.** way **d.** stay **/ Regrouping: 1a.** 52 tens **b.** 33 tens **c.** 47 tens **d.** 24 tens **2a.** 34 **b.** 43 **/Chance: a.** yellow **b.** blue **c.** white **d.** green
Unit 26	**Understanding: a.** grandma **b.** makes tea and scones **/ Responding:** Answers will vary. Parent. **Grammar: a.** past **b.** under **c.** in **d.** near **e.** on **f.** after **/ Spelling:** Parent. **/ Word Building:** bay, lay, play, clay, tray, sway, ray, away, today, stay, pay, day **/ Science and Technology:** Answers will vary. Definitely: doctors, dentists, teachers, accountants, students, police. **Multiplication: 1.** 3 x 4=12 **2a.** 15 **b.** 30 **c.** 14 **d.** 24 **e.** 40 **f.** 40 **g.** 18 **h.** 45 **/ Division: 1.** 9 : 3 = 3 **2a.** 6 **b.** 4 **c.** 8 **d.** 10 **e.** 3 **f.** 8 **g.** 6 **h.** 9
Unit 27	**Understanding: a.** older than the author. **b.** in Canberra. **/ Responding:** Answers will vary. Parent. **Punctuation: a. M**y mum likes to visit **C**anberra and **M**elbourne ⊙ **b. I**f you won a trip to **E**ngland, would you take your sister**?** **c. L**ast weekend, **W**ill and **K**ate visited grandma in **S**ydney ⊙ **/ Spelling:** Parent. **/ Compound Words:** Sunday, sometimes, helpless, butterfly, grasshopper, outside, microwave, woodlands, handful, highchair **/ Sentences: a.** Last week Ashlee went to Sydney. **b.** My older cousin Tom is ten years old. **c.** Mum bought her new skirt at Jo's Dresses. **Mass: a.** orange **b.** milk **c.** margarine **d.** sauce bottle **e.** shoe **/ Time: a.** 2:00 **b.** 10:30 **c.** 7:30 **d.** 6:30
Unit 28	**Reading: 1.** 12km. **2.** Tighs Hill **3.** 27km. **Spelling:** Parent. **/ Word Meanings: a.** trek - a long journey or trip, **b.** explore - to go looking **c.** extinct - no longer living **d.** character - a person in a play or book. **Sentences: a.** Last week. **b.** Before that **c.** At this time **d.** Now **e.** Meanwhile
Unit 29	**Timetable: 1.** every half an hour **2.** one hour **3.** 11 o'clock **4.** 8 stops **/ Chance: a.** certain. **b.** possible **c.** impossible **d.** likely **/ Spelling:** Parent. **/ Grammar: a.** an - an egg. **b.** The - The shops. **c.** a - a book **d.** the - the cinema **e.** an - an orange
Unit 30	**Time - Months: 1.** Thursday **2.** Saturday **3.** 3rd and 4th June **4.** Wednesday, 31st May **5.** 5 Saturdays **6.** 26th and 27th August **7.** 92 days **8.** Parent **9.** 1st September **/ Spelling:** Parent. **Sentences: a.** must/should/could **b.** would **c.** should/must/could **d.** must/should **e.** could/would Punctuation: **a.** "Did you wash that dish?" asked mum. **b.** "Have you any money?" he asked. **c.** "No! It wasn't me." he said. Á **d.** "Are you ready yet?" asked dad. **e.** "Look out!" he yelled. **f.** "Come here now!" called mum.